cooking for one

cooking for one

Contents

Breakfast

Croque-madame

2 eggs
1 tablespoon milk
3 teaspoons butter, softened
2 slices good-quality white bread
½ teaspoon dijon mustard
2 slices gruyère cheese
1 slice leg ham
1 teaspoon vegetable oil

Crack 1 egg into a wide, shallow bowl, add milk and beat lightly. Season with salt and freshly ground black pepper.

Using half the butter, butter the bread and then spread with dijon mustard. Place a slice of cheese on top of one bread slice, add a slice of ham and the remaining slice of cheese. Top with the second bread slice.

Heat vegetable oil and the remaining butter in a large non-stick frying pan (skillet) over medium heat. While the butter is melting, dip the sandwich into the egg and milk mixture, coating the bread on both sides. When the butter is sizzling but not browning, add the sandwich and cook for 1½ minutes on one side, pressing down firmly with a spatula. Turn over, cook the other side, then move the sandwich to the side of the pan. The bread should be lightly golden.

Gently break the remaining egg into the pan and fry until it is cooked to your liking. Transfer the sandwich to a plate, top with the fried egg and serve.

Makes 1 sandwich

Savoury breakfast tarts

110 g (3¾ oz/¾ cup) plain (all-purpose) flour
75 g (2½ oz) cold butter, diced
2 slices ham
1 tablespoon chopped parsley
1 medium tomato, finely chopped
4 eggs
60 ml (2 fl oz/¼ cup) cream
2 tablespoons grated parmesan cheese

Preheat oven to 200°C (400°F/Gas 6). Put flour and a pinch of salt into a food processor, add butter and process for a few seconds until mixture resembles breadcrumbs. With the motor running, add 2–3 teaspoons cold water to bring the dough together. Turn the dough out and use your hands to shape it into a ball. Wrap in plastic wrap, flatten slightly, and refrigerate for 10 minutes.

Divide dough in half and roll each half out on a floured work surface until very thin. Cut out a 16 cm (6½ inch) circle from each round and use to line two 10 cm (4 inch) tartlet tins. Press pastry gently into the flutes of the tins. Line each tin with a piece of crumpled paper and some uncooked rice. Bake the pastry for 5 minutes, then remove paper and rice and bake for a further 1 minute.

Line each pastry base with ham (cut it into pieces to make it fit neatly). Sprinkle with parsley and add tomato. Gently break two eggs into each tin. Pour half the cream over top of each tart, sprinkle with parmesan and then dust with salt and freshly ground black pepper.

Bake tarts for 10–12 minutes, or until the egg whites are set. Serve hot or cold.

Makes 2

Note: Cool leftover tart, then cover with plastic wrap and refrigerate until needed. Tart can be eaten cold or gently reheated the next day.

French toast with crispy prosciutto

1 tablespoon thickened cream or milk
1 egg
2 teaspoons caster (superfine) sugar
pinch of cinnamon
2 thick slices bread, cut in half diagonally
30 g (1 oz) butter
1 teaspoon olive oil
2-3 slices prosciutto

Combine the cream, egg, sugar and the cinnamon in a wide, shallow bowl. Soak bread in the egg mixture, a slice at a time, shaking off any excess.

Melt the butter in a large frying pan (skillet). When sizzling, add slices of bread in a single layer and cook until golden brown on both sides. Keep warm. Heat the olive oil in the same frying pan (skillet), then add prosciutto and fry until crisp. Remove and drain on paper towels. Place prosciutto on top of the French toast and serve.

Serves 1

Fried eggs and tomatoes on spring onion potato cakes

Spring onion potato cakes

150 g (5½ oz) potatoes, peeled and roughly chopped
1 egg yolk
30 g (1 oz/¼ cup) grated cheddar cheese
1 spring onion (scallion), trimmed and finely chopped
1 tablespoon finely chopped flat-leaf (Italian) parsley
1 tablespoon plain (all-purpose) flour
1 tablespoon olive oil

3 teaspoons olive oil, extra
1 garlic clove, sliced
1 roma (plum) tomato, halved lengthways
butter, for frying
1 egg

Boil potatoes in a saucepan of salted water until tender. Drain, then return potatoes to the pan over low heat to evaporate off any moisture. Remove the pan from the heat and mash the potatoes. Stir in the egg yolk, cheese, spring onions and parsley and season well. Form into 2 patty shapes. Cover and chill for 30 minutes. Tip flour onto a plate and lightly coat patties with it.

Heat the olive oil in a medium frying pan (skillet) over medium heat. Fry patties for 4–5 minutes on both sides until golden brown. Keep warm until needed.

Meanwhile, in a separate small non-stick frying pan, heat 2 teaspoons of olive oil over a low heat. Add the garlic and fry 2 minutes. Add tomato cut-side down and fry for 6-8 minutes, turning once during cooking. Remove from the pan and keep warm.

Add the remaining teaspoon of oil to the small pan and a little butter. When butter is sizzling, break egg into pan and cook for 1 minute. Turn off the heat and leave to stand for 1 minute. Serve the egg on top of the spring onion potato cakes and tomato.

Serves 1

Eggs benedict

2 eggs and 1 egg yolk, straight from the fridge
2 slices prosciutto
1 English muffin, split
50 g (2 oz) butter
2 teaspoons lemon juice

Heat grill (broiler). Put a medium frying pan (skillet) full of water over high heat. When water is bubbling, turn the heat down to a simmer. Crack an egg into a cup and slip the egg into the water. It should begin to turn opaque as it hits the water. Repeat with the other egg, keeping the two separated. Turn heat down; leave the eggs for 3 minutes.

Put the prosciutto on a baking tray, place it under the grill for 2 minutes, then turn it over and cook the other side. Toast the muffin under the grill or in a toaster.

Put the egg yolk into a small blender, put the lid on and leave the top hole open. Melt the butter in a small pan.

Start blender and pour in the butter in a steady stream through the top hole. The egg yolk should thicken straight away to make a thick sauce. Add the lemon juice and season the hollandaise with salt and black pepper.

Put muffin halves on a plate and put a slice of prosciutto on each. Lift each egg out of the water, drain and place on top of the prosciutto. Spoon a little hollandaise over each egg.

Serves 1

Note: Store any leftover hollandaise in a small bowl, cover with plastic wrap and refrigerate for up to 2 days. Shop-bought ready-made hollandaise can be used, if preferred. If you don't have a small blender, put the yolk in a small bowl and gradually whisk in the butter.

Grilled field mushrooms with garlic and chilli

2 medium field mushrooms
2 teaspoons butter, softened
1 small garlic clove, crushed
1/4 small red chilli, seeded and finely chopped
1 tablespoon finely chopped parsley
1 thick slice ciabatta
tomato chutney or relish
crème fraîche, to serve

Turn on the grill (broiler) and cover rack with a piece of foil so any juices stay with the mushrooms as they cook. Gently pull the stalks out of the mushrooms and peel off the skin.

Combine the butter, garlic, chilli and parsley and spread over insides of the mushrooms. Make sure butter is quite soft so it spreads easily. Season well.

Grill under a medium heat for about 8 minutes — they need to be cooked right through. Test the centre with the point of a knife if you are not sure.

Toast the bread, spread some tomato chutney or relish on it, then top with the mushrooms. Serve with a dollop of crème fraîche.

Serves 1

Piperade

2 teaspoons olive oil
1 small onion, thinly sliced
1 small red capsicum (pepper), seeded and cut into thin strips
1 garlic clove, crushed
2 tomatoes
pinch of cayenne pepper
2 eggs, lightly beaten
1 teaspoon butter
1 thin slice of ham, such as Bayonne
buttered toast

Heat the oil in a heavy-based frying pan (skillet) over medium heat, then add the onion. Cook for 3 minutes, or until soft. Add capsicum and garlic, cover and cook for 8 minutes, stirring frequently to stop mixture browning.

Score a cross in base of each tomato. Put in a large bowl of boiling water for 20 seconds, then drain and plunge into a bowl of cold water. Remove the tomatoes and peel the skin away from the cross. Chop the flesh and discard cores. Add the chopped tomato and the cayenne to the capsicum mixture, cover the pan and then cook for a further 5 minutes.

Uncover the pan and increase the heat. Cook for 3 minutes, or until the juices have evaporated, shaking the pan often. Season well with salt and freshly ground black pepper. Add the eggs and scramble into mixture until just cooked.

Heat butter in a small frying pan over a medium heat; fry ham. To serve, place piperade and cooked ham on top of the buttered toast.

Serves 1

Mushroom omelette with chorizo

30 g (1 oz) butter
½ medium chorizo sausage, sliced
50 g (1¾ oz) mushrooms, finely sliced
3 eggs
1 tablespoon finely chopped chives

Heat half of the butter in a small omelette pan or frying pan (skillet) over a medium heat. Add the chorizo and fry for 5 minutes, or until golden. Remove from the pan using a slotted spoon. Add the mushrooms to the pan and cook, stirring frequently, for about 4 minutes, or until soft. Add to the chorizo.

Break eggs into a bowl and season with salt and freshly ground black pepper. Add the chives and beat lightly with a fork.

Put remaining butter in the pan and melt over medium heat until foaming. Add eggs and cook for 20 seconds, in which time they will start to set on the bottom, then quickly stir mixture with a fork. Work quickly, drawing away some of the cooked egg from bottom of the pan and allowing some of the uncooked egg to set, tilting the pan a little as you go. Once eggs are mostly set, arrange mushrooms and the chorizo on top. Cook for a further 1 minute, if necessary. Tip omelette out onto a plate and serve.

Serves 1

Scrambled eggs and salmon on brioche

2 fresh eggs
2 tablespoons cream
1 tablespoon unsalted butter
60 g (2¼ oz) smoked salmon, sliced
1 teaspoon finely chopped dill
1 individual brioche bun or 1 croissant, warmed

Crack the eggs into a bowl, add the cream and beat thoroughly. Season with some salt and freshly ground black pepper.

Melt butter in a small non-stick frying pan (skillet). When it starts to sizzle, add the eggs and turn the heat down to low. Using a flat-ended wooden spoon, push the mixture around until it starts to set, then add salmon and dill. Continue to cook, gently folding salmon and dill through mixture until the eggs are mostly cooked, and just a little liquid is left in the pan.

Slice the top off the brioche (or the croissant), scoop out some of the filling, then pile the scrambled eggs on top and serve.

Serves 1

Cheese and herb cornbread with scrambled eggs

Cornbread

185 g (6½ oz/1¼ cups) self-raising flour
1 tablespoon caster (superfine) sugar
2 teaspoons baking powder
½ teaspoon salt
110 g (3¾ oz/¾ cup) fine polenta
60 g (2¼ oz/½ cup) grated cheddar cheese
large handful mixed herbs (chives, dill, parsley), chopped
2 eggs
250 ml (9 fl oz/1 cup) buttermilk
80 ml (2½ fl oz/⅓ cup) macadamia or olive oil

Scrambled eggs

2 eggs
2 tablespoons cream
small basil leaves, to garnish

Note: Leftover cornbread is good toasted. It will keep for several days in an airtight container and can also be frozen. Cut the bread into thick slices, wrap each slice individually in plastic wrap and freeze in an airtight container for up to 1 month.

Preheat oven to 180°C (350°F/Gas 4). Grease a 20 x 10 cm (8 x 4 inch) loaf (bar) tin. Sift the flour, sugar, baking powder and the salt into a bowl. Add the polenta, cheddar, herbs, the eggs, buttermilk and oil and mix to combine. Spoon mixture into loaf (bar) tin. Bake for 45 minutes, or until a skewer inserted in centre comes out clean. Remove from tin.

To make one serve of the scrambled eggs, whisk the eggs and cream and season with salt and pepper. Pour the mixture into a small non-stick frying pan (skillet) and cook over a low heat, stirring occasionally until the egg is just set. (The more you stir the eggs, the more scrambled they become.) Serve the scrambled eggs with a slice of buttered cornbread. Sprinkle with basil leaves.

Serves 1

Banana bread

3 ripe bananas, well mashed
2 eggs, well beaten
2 teaspoons grated orange zest
300 g (10½ oz/2 cups) plain (all-purpose) flour
1 teaspoon ground cinnamon
½ teaspoon salt
1 teaspoon bicarbonate of soda (baking soda)
170 g (6 oz/¾ cup) caster (superfine) sugar
75 g (2½ oz/¾ cup) walnuts, coarsely chopped

Note: Leftover banana bread will keep for several days in an airtight container. To freeze, cut bread into thick slices, wrap them individually in plastic wrap and freeze in an airtight container for up to 1 month.

Preheat oven to 180°C (350°F/Gas 4). Grease a 17 x 8 cm (7 x 3 inch) loaf (bar) tin.

Combine the bananas, eggs and the orange zest in a large bowl. Sift in the flour, cinnamon, salt and bicarbonate of soda, mix, then add the sugar and walnuts. Mix thoroughly, then tip into the prepared tin. Bake for 1 hour and 10 minutes, or until a skewer inserted into centre comes out clean.

Serve warm or allow to cool, then toast and serve buttered.

Makes 1 loaf

Creamed rice with minted citrus compote

65 g (2¼ oz/⅓ cup) basmati rice
250 ml (9 fl oz/1 cup) milk
2 cardamom pods, bruised
small piece cinnamon stick
1 clove
1–1½ tablespoons honey, to taste
½ teaspoon natural vanilla extract

Minted citrus compote
½ ruby grapefruit, peeled and segmented
1 small orange, peeled and segmented
1 tablespoon orange juice
¼ teaspoon grated lime zest
1 tablespoon honey
2 fresh mint leaves, finely chopped

Note: Leftover creamy rice will keep for 2 days, covered in the refrigerator. Reheat gently or serve at room temperature, if desired.

Cook the rice in a small saucepan of boiling water for 12 minutes, stirring occasionally. Drain and cool.

Return the rice to the saucepan and add the milk, cardamom pods, cinnamon stick and clove. Slowly bring to the boil. Reduce the heat to low and simmer for 15 minutes, stirring occasionally, until the milk is absorbed and the rice is creamy. Remove the spices, then stir in the honey, to taste, and the vanilla.

To make the compote, combine the ruby grapefruit, orange, orange juice, lime zest, honey and mint and mix until the honey has dissolved. Serve with the rice.

Serves 1

Cinnamon porridge with caramel figs and cream

50 g (1¾ oz /½ cup) rolled (porridge) oats
pinch ground cinnamon
1 tablespoon butter
2 tablespoons brown sugar
80 ml (2½ fl oz/⅓ cup) cream
1 fresh fig, halved
milk, to serve
thick (double/heavy) cream, to serve

Note: Store leftover caramel sauce in a covered bowl in the refrigerator for up to 5 days.

Place the oats, 250 ml (9 fl oz/1 cup) water and cinnamon in a saucepan. Stir over a medium heat for 5 minutes, or until the porridge becomes thick and smooth. Set the porridge aside.

Melt the butter in a small frying pan (skillet), add all but 1 teaspoon of the brown sugar and stir until it dissolves. Stir in the cream and bring to the boil, then simmer for 5 minutes, or until the sauce starts to thicken slightly.

Place the fig halves onto a baking tray, sprinkle with the remaining teaspoon of sugar and grill (broil) until the sugar is melted.

Spoon the porridge into a bowl, add a little milk, then top with the fig halves, some caramel sauce and a generous dollop of thick cream.

Serves 1

Healthy nut and seed muesli

100 g (3½ oz/6 cups) puffed corn
150 g (5½ oz/1½ cups) rolled oats
100 g (3½ oz/1 cup) pecans, roughly chopped
135 g (4¾ oz/1 cup) raw macadamia nuts, roughly chopped
110 g (3¾ oz/2 cups) flaked coconut
200 g packet (7 oz/1¾ cups) LSA (linseed, sunflower and almond mix)
100 g (3½ oz/1⅓ cups) dried apples, chopped
200 g packet (6½ oz/1⅓ cups) dried apricots, chopped
125 g (4½ oz/1 cup) dried pears, chopped
125 ml (4 fl oz/½ cup) maple syrup
1 teaspoon natural vanilla extract

Preheat oven to 160°C (315°F/Gas 2-3). Place puffed corn, rolled oats, pecans, macadamia nuts, coconut, LSA, apples, apricots and pears in a large bowl and mix to combine.

Place maple syrup and vanilla in a small saucepan and cook over a low heat for 1 minute, or until maple syrup becomes easy to pour. Pour maple syrup over mixture and toss thoroughly to coat.

Divide the muesli mixture between two large ceramic non-stick baking dishes. Bake for 30 minutes, turning frequently, until the muesli is lightly toasted. Let the mixture cool before storing it in an airtight container.

Makes 1.2 kg (2 lb 10 oz/15 cups)

Blueberry pancakes

125 ml (4 fl oz/1/2 cup) buttermilk
1 egg
2 teaspoons melted butter
1/2 teaspoon natural vanilla extract
75 g (2 1/2 oz/1/2 cup) plain (all-purpose) flour
1 teaspoon baking powder
pinch salt
1 small ripe banana, mashed
50 g (1 3/4 oz/1/3 cup) blueberries
vegetable oil or butter, for cooking
maple syrup, to serve

Note: Refrigerate remaining cooled pancakes between sheets of baking paper and cover with plastic wrap. They will keep for 1 day in the fridge. Gently warm in a microwave to serve.

Put the buttermilk, egg, butter and vanilla essence in a bowl and whisk together. Sift in the flour, baking powder and salt, then stir, making sure not to over-blend as the batter should be lumpy. Add the fruit.

Heat oil in a frying pan (skillet) over medium heat. Add 80 ml (2 1/2 fl oz/1/3 cup) of batter to the pan for each pancake. Cook for 3 minutes, or until pancakes are golden brown on the bottom, then turn over and cook for 1 minute more. Repeat with remaining batter, keeping the cooked pancakes warm. For a single serve, place one or two pancakes on a plate and drizzle with maple syrup.

Makes about 4 pancakes

Grilled stone fruits with cinnamon toast

1 tablespoon low-fat margarine
2 large pinches ground cinnamon
1 thick slice good-quality brioche
1 ripe plum, halved and stones removed
1 ripe nectarine, halved and stones removed
2 teaspoons warmed honey

Note: Tinned plums or apricots may be used in place of fresh stone fruits.

Preheat grill. Place margarine and a pinch of ground cinnamon in a small bowl and mix until well combined. Grill (broil) brioche slice on one side until golden. Spread the other side with half the cinnamon spread, then grill until golden. Keep warm in the oven.

Brush the plum and nectarine halves with the remaining spread and cook under the grill or on a ridged grill plate, until the spread is bubbling and the fruit is tinged at the edges.

Place plum and nectarine halves on the toasted brioche, dust with the remaining cinnamon and drizzle with the warmed honey.

Serves 1

Raspberry breakfast crepes

150 g (5½ oz/1 cup) plain (all-purpose) flour
pinch of salt
1 teaspoon sugar
1 egg, lightly beaten
250 ml (9 fl oz/1 cup) milk
2 teaspoons melted butter
fresh or frozen and defrosted raspberries
icing (confectioners') sugar, for dusting
maple syrup or honey, to serve

Note: Store leftover crepes interleaved with baking paper in the refrigerator for 2 days. Or, freeze in an airtight container for up to 1 month. Defrost as needed and reheat in a microwave.

Sift flour, salt and sugar into a bowl and make a well in the centre. Whisk the egg and milk together with 60 ml (2 fl oz/¼ cup) water. Slowly pour this mixture into the well, whisking all the time to incorporate the flour and make a smooth batter. Stir in melted butter. Cover and refrigerate for 20 minutes.

Heat a 20 cm/8 inch (across base) crepe pan or a small non-stick frying pan (skillet) over medium heat and lightly grease. Pour in enough batter to coat base of the pan in a thin, even layer. Tip out any excess. Cook for 1 minute, or until crepe starts to come away from side of the pan. Turn and cook on other side for 1 minute more until just golden. Repeat the process until all the batter is used, stacking the crepes on a plate with baking paper between them and covering them with foil to keep them warm.

To make one serve, put one crepe on a serving plate. Arrange some of the raspberries on a quarter of the crepe. Fold crepe in half, then in half again, so that raspberries are wrapped in a little triangular pocket. Repeat with one or two more crepes and raspberries. Dust with icing sugar and drizzle with maple syrup or honey.

Makes 6 crepes

Mixed berry couscous

45 g (1 1/2 oz/1/4 cup) couscous
125 ml (4 fl oz/1/2 cup) apple and cranberry juice
small piece cinnamon stick
a handful of mixed berries, such as raspberries, blueberries, blackberries, halved strawberries, fresh or frozen and defrosted
1/8 teaspoon lime zest
1/8 teaspoon orange zest
thick Greek-style yoghurt, to serve
golden syrup, to drizzle
mint leaves, to garnish

Put couscous in a serving bowl. Place apple and cranberry juice in a small saucepan with the cinnamon stick. Bring to the boil, remove from heat and pour over the couscous. Cover with plastic wrap and allow to stand for 5 minutes, or until all the liquid has been absorbed. Discard cinnamon.

Separate the grains of the couscous with a fork, add the mixed berries, lime zest and orange zest and fold through gently. Serve with a generous dollop of yoghurt and a drizzle of golden syrup. Garnish with mint leaves.

Serves 1

Ginger and ricotta flatcakes with fresh honeycomb

35 g (1 1/4 oz/1/4 cup) wholemeal (whole wheat) flour
1/2 teaspoon baking powder
1/2 teaspoon ground ginger
2 teaspoons caster (superfine) sugar
15 g (1/2 oz/1/4 cup) flaked coconut, toasted
1 egg, separated
90 g (3 1/4 oz/1/3 cup) ricotta cheese
80 ml (2 1/2 fl oz/1/3 cup) milk
ricotta, extra, to serve
sliced banana, to serve
fresh honeycomb

Note: Leftover pancakes will keep covered and refrigerated for 1 day. Gently reheat in a microwave.

Sift the flour, baking powder, fresh ginger and sugar into a small bowl. Return flour husks to the bowl, stir in the coconut and make a well in the centre. Add the combined egg yolk, the ricotta and milk. Mix until smooth.

Beat egg white until soft peaks form, then fold into the pancake mixture.

Heat a non-stick frying pan (skillet) over low heat and brush lightly with melted butter or oil. Pour 80 ml (2 1/2 fl oz/1/3 cup) of batter into the pan, swirling gently to create an even pancake. Cook until bubbles appear on the surface. Flip and cook the other side for 1 minute, or until golden. Repeat until all the batter is used up.

For a single serve, stack pancakes on a plate and top with a dollop of ricotta, some sliced banana and a large piece of fresh honeycomb.

Makes 4

Lunch

Thai chicken sausage rolls

250 g (9 oz) minced (ground) chicken
½ teaspoon ground cumin
½ teaspoon ground coriander
1 tablespoon sweet chilli sauce
1 tablespoon chopped coriander (cilantro) leaves
40 g (1½ oz/½ cup) fresh breadcrumbs
1 sheet frozen puff pastry, thawed
1 small egg, lightly beaten
2 teaspoons sesame seeds
baby rocket (arugula) leaves, to serve
sweet chilli sauce, extra, for dipping

Notes: Leftover rolls will keep, covered and refrigerated for 1 day. Reheat in a 180°C (350°F/Gas 4) oven for about 10 minutes until warmed through.

Preheat the oven to 200°C (400°F/Gas 6). Combine the chicken, cumin, coriander, chilli sauce, coriander leaves and breadcrumbs in a bowl.

Spread mixture along one edge of pastry sheet and roll up to conceal the filling. Place roll seam-side down on a tray lined with baking paper, brush lightly with the beaten egg and then sprinkle with the sesame seeds. Bake for 30 minutes, or until golden and cooked through. Slice the roll into 4 pieces and then serve with rocket and sweet chilli sauce.

Makes 4 sausage rolls

Fattoush with fried haloumi

½ Lebanese (short) cucumber
1 pitta bread
1 small garlic clove, crushed
1 tablespoon lemon juice
3 tablespoons olive oil
1 spring onion (scallion), sliced
1 tomato, diced
½ green capsicum (pepper), diced
1 large handful flat-leaf (Italian) parsley, chopped
1 tablespoon chopped mint
1 tablespoon chopped oregano
125 g (4 oz) haloumi cheese, cut into 2 slices
sumac, optional

Preheat grill (broiler). Peel cucumber, cut it into half lengthways, then cut each piece into thick slices. Put these in a sieve and sprinkle with a little salt to help draw out any excess liquid, which would make the salad soggy.

Split pitta bread in half and toast on both sides to make the bread crisp, then break it into small pieces. Mix garlic, lemon juice and 2 tablespoons of the oil to make a dressing. Rinse and drain the cucumber.

Put cucumber, spring onion, tomato, green capsicum, parsley, mint and oregano in a serving bowl. Add the dressing and toss together well.

Heat remaining tablespoon of oil in a non-stick frying pan (skillet) and fry the haloumi cheese on both sides until it is browned. Scatter bread over the salad and fold it through.

Serve the fattoush with the slices of haloumi on top. Sprinkle with a little sumac, if you like.

Serves 1

Spanish omelette with smoked salmon

1 tablespoon olive oil
150 g (5½ oz) potatoes, peeled and cubed
1 small onion, finely chopped
2 eggs
1 tablespoon chopped dill
2 slices smoked salmon
1 tablespoon mascarpone cheese
1 large handful salad leaves

Heat the oil in a small non-stick frying pan (skillet) and add the potato cubes. Fry them gently, stirring so they brown on all sides and cook through to the middle. This should take 10 minutes. Cut a cube open to see if it is cooked through completely.

When potato is cooked, add the onion and cook gently for a few minutes until it is translucent and soft. Preheat the grill (broiler).

When onion is almost ready, break the eggs into a bowl and whisk them with salt, freshly ground pepper and dill.

Tear smoked salmon into pieces and add it to frying pan. Add mascarpone in blobs. Using a spatula, pull mixture into centre of the pan and level it off. Pour the eggs over the top and cook for 5–10 minutes, or until the omelette is just set.

Put frying pan under the grill for a minute or two to lightly brown top of omelette. Slide the omelette out of the frying pan (skillet) and cut into wedges. Arrange salad leaves on a plate and top with wedges of omelette.

Serves 1

Bagel with smoked salmon and caper salsa

1 plain or rye bagel
30 g (1 oz) neufchatel cream cheese
2–3 slices smoked salmon
1 spring onion (scallion), chopped
1 roma (plum) tomato, finely chopped
2 teaspoons baby capers
2 teaspoons finely chopped fresh dill
2 teaspoons lemon juice
1 teaspoon extra virgin olive oil

Cut the bagel in half and spread the base generously with cream cheese, then top with the salmon slices.

Combine the spring onion, tomato, capers, dill, lemon juice and olive oil in a bowl. Pile this mixture onto the salmon and serve.

Serves 1

Wild rice salad

50 g (1¾ oz/¼ cup) wild rice
250 ml (9 fl oz/1 cup) chicken stock
2 teaspoons butter
50 g (1¾ oz/¼ cup) basmati rice
1 slice bacon, rind removed, chopped and cooked
50 g (1¾ oz/⅓ cup) currants
30 g (1¾ oz/¼ cup) slivered almonds, toasted
small handful parsley, chopped
2 spring onions (scallions), finely sliced
grated zest and juice of ½ a lemon
olive oil, to drizzle
lemon wedge, to serve

Note: Cover and refrigerate any leftover salad. It can be eaten cold or at room temperature the next day.

Put the wild rice, stock and butter in a saucepan, bring to the boil and cook, covered, over a low heat for 1 hour. Drain well.

Put the basmati rice in a separate small saucepan with cold water and bring to the boil. Cook at a simmer for 12 minutes, then drain. Mix with the cooked wild rice and leave to cool.

Combine the rice mixture with the bacon, currants, almonds, parsley, spring onion, lemon zest and juice. Season well, drizzle with olive oil and serve with lemon wedges.

Serves 1

Tomato caponata with mozzarella

1 small eggplant (aubergine), cubed
olive oil, for frying
1 small onion, cubed
1 celery stalk, sliced
1 small red capsicum (pepper), seeded and cubed
2 ripe roma (plum) tomatoes, chopped
125 g (4 oz) red and 125 g (4 oz) yellow cherry tomatoes, halved
1 tablespoon red wine vinegar
¼ teaspoon sugar
1 tablespoon capers, rinsed
40 g (1½ oz/⅓ cup) unpitted black olives
100 g (3½ oz/⅔ cup) fresh mozzarella cheese, chopped
a small handful parsley, roughly chopped
green salad, to serve
bread, to mop up juices

Note: Cover and refrigerate leftover caponata. Use within 4 days. It is delicious eaten at room temperature. The flavour improves on keeping. It is also good served over pasta or rice.

Cook eggplant in boiling salted water for 1 minute; drain and cool. Squeeze out excess moisture with your hands.

Heat 2 tablespoons of oil in a large frying pan (skillet), add eggplant and brown on all sides over a high heat, adding more oil if needed. When cooked, drain on paper towels.

Add a little more oil to pan, reduce heat and cook onion and celery for 5 minutes, or until soft but not brown. Add the red capsicum and cook for 2 minutes. Add the chopped tomato and a couple of tablespoons of water. Simmer mixture for 5 minutes, or until it is quite dry. Add cherry tomatoes.

Season the mixture well with black pepper. Add red wine vinegar, sugar, capers and olives; cook for 5 minutes over a low heat. Add eggplant and cook for 5–10 minutes to heat.

Take the mixture off the heat and leave to cool. Toss mozzarella and parsley through the caponata. Pile onto a serving plate. Serve with a green salad and some bread to mop up the juices.

Serves 1

Creamy egg salad

4 large eggs, plus 1 egg yolk
1 tablespoon lemon juice
1 teaspoon dijon mustard
60 ml (2 fl oz/¼ cup) olive oil
60 ml (2 fl oz/¼ cup) safflower oil
1 tablespoon chopped dill
1 tablespoon crème fraîche or sour cream
1 tablespoon capers, rinsed and drained
a handful mustard or salad cress

Note: Leftover egg salad will keep for 1 day, covered and refrigerated. Leftover mayonnaise dressing will keep for up to 5 days, covered and refrigerated. If preferred, use a good-quality bought mayonnaise. If you don't have a small food processor or blender, use a hand-held blender or make the mayonnaise in a small bowl using a whisk.

Put the whole eggs in a saucepan of water. Bring to the boil and simmer for 10 minutes. Drain, then cool under cold water and peel.

To make dressing, place egg yolk, a teaspoon of lemon juice and the dijon mustard in a small food processor or blender and season. With the motor running, slowly add oils, drop by drop, increasing to a thin, steady stream as the mixture thickens. Add remaining lemon juice, to taste. Thin with a little hot water, if too thick.

When combined, put the mayonnaise in a medium bowl, and stir in the dill, crème fraîche and capers.

Chop eggs and gently fold in enough of the mayonnaise to coat the eggs. For a single serve put a portion in a bowl, sprinkle over just the green tips of the mustard cress and serve.

Serves 1

Tomato and pesto bruschetta

2 thick slices ciabatta
olive oil, for brushing
about 1 tablespoon pesto
2 ripe roma (plum) tomatoes
1 tablespoon mascarpone cheese

Preheat the grill (broiler) to its highest setting. To make bruschetta, brush both sides of each piece of bread with a little olive oil and put the bread on a baking tray. Grill for 2 minutes on each side, or until crisp and golden brown. Remove from the tray.

Spread a teaspoon of the pesto over each piece of bruschetta. Slice the tomatoes into four pieces lengthways and drain briefly on paper towels; this will stop the juice from the tomatoes making the bruschetta soggy. Put the tomato slices on the baking tray.

Grill tomato for about 4–5 minutes; it will start to cook and brown at the edges. When the tomato is cooked, layer four slices onto each piece of the bruschetta. Return bruschetta to the tray; grill for a further 1 minute to heat through. Add a dollop of the mascarpone and a little more pesto to each piece of bruschetta. Serve hot.

Serves 1

Chargrilled asparagus with salsa

1 egg
2 teaspoons milk
1 tablespoon olive oil
1 corn cob
½ small red onion, diced
½ small red capsicum (pepper), finely chopped
2 teaspoons chopped fresh thyme
2 teaspoons balsamic vinegar
6 fresh asparagus spears
olive oil, extra, to brush
toasted wholegrain bread, to serve

Beat egg and milk to combine. Heat 1 teaspoon of oil in a small non-stick frying pan (skillet), add egg in a thin layer and cook over a medium heat until just set. Flip and cook the other side. Remove and allow to cool, then roll up and cut into thin slices.

Cook the corn on a chargrill (griddle) or in boiling water, until tender. Set aside to cool slightly, then slice off the corn kernels. Make the salsa by gently combining the corn, onion, capsicum, thyme, remaining olive oil and balsamic vinegar.

Trim away any woody ends from the asparagus, lightly brush with extra olive oil and cook on the chargrill until tender. Serve asparagus topped with salsa and egg slices, accompanied by buttered, toasted wholegrain bread.

Serves 1

Fried egg and red onion wrap

2 teaspoons olive oil
1 small red onion, thickly sliced
½ small red capsicum (pepper), sliced
3 teaspoons balsamic vinegar
1 egg
1 lavash bread
1 tablespoon sour cream
sweet chilli sauce, to drizzle

Heat olive oil in a medium non-stick frying pan (skillet); add onion. Cook slowly, stirring occasionally until it softens and turns translucent. Add the red capsicum and continue cooking until both the onion and capsicum are soft. Increase heat and stir for a minute or two, or until vegetables start to brown. Stir in balsamic vinegar. Remove the mixture from the pan; keep warm.

Carefully break the egg into the frying pan. Cook over a gentle heat until the egg is just set.

Heat lavash bread in a microwave or under a grill (broiler) for a few seconds (it should be soft and warm). Lay the bread out on a board, spread the sour cream onto the centre, then drizzle with a little chilli sauce. Heap onion and capsicum mixture on and top with an egg. Season with salt and pepper. Fold in one short end of the lavash bread and then roll up lengthways.

Serves 1

Mediterranean blt

1 vine-ripened tomato, halved longthways
4 unpeeled garlic cloves
2 teaspoons extra virgin olive oil
about 6 large basil leaves
1 thick slice of Italian woodfired bread
2 slices provolone cheese
2 slices mortadella
1 small handful rocket (arugula)
extra virgin olive oil, extra
balsamic vinegar

Preheat the oven to 200°C (400°F/Gas 6). Place the tomato and garlic in a small roasting pan. Drizzle with olive oil and sprinkle with sea salt and cracked black pepper. Roast for about 25 minutes, or until the garlic is soft and the tomato is slightly dried. Add the basil leaves and continue cooking for 5 minutes, or until the leaves are crisp. Remove from the oven.

Lightly toast the bread on both sides. Peel the roasted garlic cloves and spread half onto the toast. Top with provolone, mortadella, rocket, basil and roasted tomato. Sprinkle with the remaining roasted garlic, drizzle with extra olive oil and some balsamic vinegar and serve immediately.

Serves 1

Mini sweet potato and leek frittatas

300 g (10½ oz) orange sweet potato, peeled
1 teaspoon olive oil
2 teaspoons butter
½ small leek, white part only, thinly sliced
1 garlic clove, crushed
75 g (2½ oz/½ cup) feta cheese, crumbled
3 eggs
60 ml (2 fl oz/¼ cup) pouring cream

Note: The remaining frittatas can be covered and refrigerated for up to 2 days. Eat at room temperature or reheat in a 180°C (350°F/Gas 4) oven for 10 minutes.

Preheat oven to 180°C (350°F/Gas 4). Grease four 185 ml (¾ cup) muffin tin holes. Line bases with small rounds of baking paper. Cut sweet potato into small cubes. Boil, steam or microwave until tender. Drain well; set aside.

Heat the oil and butter in a frying pan (skillet), add leek and cook for about 5 minutes, stirring occasionally, or until soft and lightly golden. Add garlic and cook for a further 1 minute. Cool, then stir in the feta and sweet potato. Divide mixture evenly among the muffin holes.

Whisk eggs and cream together, and season with salt and freshly ground black pepper. Pour egg mixture into each hole until three-quarters filled, pressing the vegetables down gently. Bake for 20 minutes, or until golden and set. Leave in the tin for 5 minutes, then ease out with a knife. Serve while warm. Cool remaining frittatas on a wire rack.

Makes 4

Thai chicken with glass noodles

3 tablespoons coconut cream
3 teaspoons fish sauce
3 teaspoons grated palm sugar
1 small chicken breast, skinned and cut into thin shreds
60 g (2¼ oz) glass noodles
1 lemongrass stem
1 makrut (kaffir lime) leaf
½ small red onion, finely chopped
a small handful coriander (cilantro) leaves, chopped
a small handful mint, chopped
¼—½ red chilli, seeded and finely sliced
¼ green bird's eye chilli, seeded and finely sliced
2 teaspoons roasted peanuts, chopped
1 lime, halved

Mix coconut cream, fish sauce and palm sugar in a small pan or a wok and bring to the boil. Add the chicken and simmer until it is cooked through. This should only take a minute if you stir it a couple of times. Leave chicken to cool in the sauce. Soak the noodles in boiling water for a minute or two — they should turn translucent and soft when ready. Drain, then, using a pair of scissors, cut into shorter lengths.

Peel lemongrass until you reach the first purplish ring, then trim off root. Make two or three cuts down through the bulb-like root, finely slice across it until it starts to get harder, then throw the hard top piece away. Pull stem out of lime leaf by folding the leaf in half, shiny side inwards, and pulling down on the stalk. Roll up tightly, then slice very finely across.

Place the ingredients, except the lime, in a deep bowl with the noodles and chicken, with its sauce. Toss well to combine. Squeeze lime juice over the dish and toss again.

Serves 1

Steak baguette with rocket and mustardy mayo

1 tablespoon olive oil, plus extra for frying
1 small red onion, sliced
1 teaspoon brown sugar
2 teaspoons balsamic vinegar
1 teaspoon thyme
1 teaspoon dijon mustard
1 tablespoon mayonnaise
small handful rocket (arugula) leaves
85 g (3 oz) beef fillet steak
1 thick baguette, cut in half, or 2 thick slices of good-quality bread
1 small tomato, sliced

Note: Leftover onion jam will keep, covered and refrigerated, for up to 5 days.

Heat oil in a small saucepan. Add the onion and cook very slowly, with the lid on, stirring occasionally, until onion is soft but not brown. This could take up to 15 minutes. Remove the lid, add sugar and vinegar and cook a further 10 minutes, or until the onion is soft and just browned. Remove pan from stove; stir in thyme.

To make mustardy mayo, combine mustard and mayonnaise in a bowl.

Halve beef fillet through the centre to butterfly out and then flatten it out a bit to make a thin slice. Heat a little of the extra oil in a small frying pan (skillet) over high heat and cook the steak for 2 minutes on each side, or to the degree of doneness you like. Season to taste.

To serve, spread the baguette with the mustardy mayo. Then fill and layer the bread with some onion jam, rocket leaves, steak and sliced tomatoes.

Serves 1

Chargrilled baby octopus

500 g (1 lb 2 oz) baby octopus
250 ml (9 fl oz/1 cup) red wine
2 tablespoons balsamic vinegar
1 tablespoon soy sauce
60 ml (2 fl oz/¼ cup) sweet chilli sauce
small handful Thai basil leaves, to serve

Note: Keep any leftover octopus in the refrigerator for 1 day in a covered, non-metallic container. Reheat gently.

Clean and remove the beak from the octopus. Place octopus, red wine and balsamic vinegar in a medium non-aluminium saucepan and bring to the boil. Reduce heat; simmer 15 minutes, or until just tender. Drain and transfer to a bowl. Add soy sauce and sweet chilli sauce.

Heat a barbecue chargrill (griddle) to high and cook the octopus until it is sticky and slightly charred. Serve on a bed of Thai basil leaves.

Serves 1

Beef salad with sweet and sour cucumber

½ Lebanese (short) cucumber
2 teaspoons caster (superfine) sugar
2 tablespoons red wine vinegar
2 teaspoons oil
85 g (3 oz) beef fillet steak, cut into even strips
2 spring onions (scallions), chopped
1 garlic clove, crushed
2 teaspoons grated ginger
1 tablespoon soy sauce
1 handful mixed lettuce leaves

Halve cucumber lengthways and slice thinly. Put in a colander, sprinkle with salt and leave for 10 minutes. This will draw out any excess moisture and stop the final flavour tasting watery.

Meanwhile, put 1 teaspoon each of sugar and vinegar in a bowl; stir until sugar dissolves. Rinse the salt off the cucumber and drain well. Pat with paper towels to soak up any excess moisture. Combine cucumber with the vinegar mixture.

Heat oil in a frying pan (skillet) or wok until it is almost smoking. Add steak and fry for 1 minute. Add spring onion and fry for another minute. Add the garlic and the ginger, toss everything around once, then add the soy sauce and the remaining sugar and vinegar. Cook until sauce turns sticky. Quickly remove from the heat.

Put the lettuce leaves on a plate and top with the beef mixture. Scatter the cucumber on top.

Serves 1

Individual herbed lemon ricotta

125 g (4½ oz/½ cup) ricotta cheese

Dressing
2 tablespoons olive oil
1 small garlic clove, crushed
1 teaspoon grated lemon zest
2 teaspoons lemon juice
1 teaspoon balsamic vinegar
1 tablespoon chopped parsley

2–3 semi-dried (sun-blushed) tomatoes, roughly chopped
crusty bread, to serve

Lightly grease and line a 125 ml (4 fl oz/½ cup) ramekin with plastic wrap. Put the ricotta in the mould and press down firmly. Cover with plastic wrap and refrigerate for 2 hours.

Preheat the oven to 220°C (425°F/Gas 7). Unmould the ricotta onto a small tray lined with baking paper and bake for 20 minutes, or until golden.

To make the dressing, combine all the ingredients in a bowl. Place the ricotta on a serving plate. Scatter over the tomatoes and spoon a little of the dressing around, drizzling a little over the top. Serve with crusty bread.

Serves 1

Caesar salad

½ cos (romaine) lettuce
4 thin slices baguette
150 ml (5 fl oz) olive oil
1 bacon slice, rind cut off, chopped
1 egg yolk
1 small garlic clove, crushed
1 anchovy fillet
2—3 teaspoons lemon juice
worcestershire sauce, to taste
a lump of parmesan cheese

Note: If you don't have a small blender, use a hand-held blender, or make the mayonnaise in a small bowl, using a whisk. Leftover mayonnaise will keep, covered and refrigerated, for up to 5 days. If preferred, instead of making your own, use a good-quality shop-bought mayonnaise or a Caesar salad dressing. Tear cos lettuce into pieces and put in a serving bowl.

Preheat grill (broiler).

Lightly brush baguette slices on both sides with some of the oil and grill until golden brown all over. Leave to cool.

Grill bacon until it browns and then sprinkle it over the bowl of lettuce.

Put egg yolk, garlic and anchovy in a small blender; whizz for 1 minute. Then, with motor still running, add oil a few drops at a time through the top hole. As mixture thickens, add oil in a steady stream. When it has all been incorporated, add lemon juice and worcestershire sauce, to taste. Season with salt and pepper.

Using a potato peeler, make some parmesan curls by running the peeler along one edge of the cheese. Try to make the curls as thin as possible.

Pour on sufficient dressing to coat lettuce. Add the parmesan curls and toss everything together well. Serve topped with the toasted baguette.

Serves 1

Barbecued sweet chilli seafood on a banana mat

125 g (4½ oz) raw prawns (shrimp), peeled and deveined, tails left intact
80 g (2¾ oz) scallop meat
125 g (4½ oz) baby squid, cleaned and hoods cut in quarters
125 g (4½ oz) baby octopus, cleaned and beak removed
80 ml (2½ oz/⅓ cup) sweet chilli sauce
2 teaspoons fish sauce
1 tablespoon lime juice
1 tablespoon peanut oil
square of banana leaf, to serve
lime wedges, to serve

Place the seafood in a shallow, non-metallic bowl. In a separate bowl, combine the sweet chilli sauce, fish sauce, the lime juice and half of the peanut oil. Pour over seafood and mix gently to coat. Leave to marinate in a cool place for 1 hour. Drain the seafood well, reserving the marinade.

Heat the remaining oil on a barbecue hotplate. Cook seafood in batches, if necessary (depending on the size of your barbecue) over a high heat for 3–5 minutes, or until tender. Drizzle with a little of the leftover marinade during cooking.

Pile the seafood onto the banana leaf, or onto a flat plate, with lime wedges on the side.

Serves 1

Spinach and zucchini frittata

2 teaspoons olive oil
1 small red onion, thinly sliced
1 zucchini (courgette), sliced
1 small garlic clove, crushed
100 g (3½ oz) baby spinach leaves
3 eggs
1 tablespoon cream
40 g (1½ oz/⅓ cup) emmental cheese, grated

Heat the oil in a small non-stick frying pan (skillet) and fry the onion and zucchini over medium heat until pale golden brown. Add garlic and cook 1 minute. Add the spinach and cook until leaves have wilted and excess moisture has evaporated. (If you don't do this, your frittata will be soggy in the middle.) Shake pan to get an even layer of mixture. Reduce heat to low.

Beat eggs and cream together and season with salt and pepper. Stir in half the cheese and pour the mixture over the spinach. Cook the bottom of the frittata for about 4 minutes, or until the egg is just set. While you are doing this, turn on the grill (broiler). When the bottom of the frittata is set, scatter on the rest of the cheese and put the frying pan under the grill to cook the top.

Turn the frittata out of the frying pan after leaving it to set for a minute. Cut it into wedges to serve.

Serves 1

Note: Cover and refrigerate leftover frittata wedges for 1 day.

Mushrooms with marinated feta

1 oxheart or vine-ripened tomato
5—6 fresh asparagus spears
45 g (1½ oz⅓ cup) marinated feta cheese
1½ tablespoons extra virgin olive oil
1 teaspoon grated lemon zest
1 small garlic clove, crushed
1 tablespoon lemon juice
2 medium field mushrooms, brushed clean and stems removed
1 egg
fresh oregano, to garnish

Cut tomato into thick slices. Trim the ends from the asparagus.

Drain the feta and put the marinade in a small non-metallic bowl. Whisk in the olive oil, lemon zest, garlic and lemon juice. Season with cracked black pepper.

Place the mushrooms and tomato slices in a shallow dish and pour the oil mixture over them. Toss gently to coat. Marinate for 15 minutes. Drain mushrooms, reserving the marinade, and cook with the tomato, on a lightly oiled barbecue grill plate until tender.

Add asparagus towards the end of cooking, and lastly the egg. Cook and turn asparagus until tender and the egg has set. Place the mushrooms on a plate, top with asparagus spears, slices of tomato, the egg and the feta. Drizzle with a little oil marinade and garnish with a few oregano leaves.

Serves 1

Toasted cheese, aïoli and ham sandwich

- 1 large piece ciabatta or Turkish bread
- 1 small garlic clove, crushed
- 2 tablespoons mayonnaise
- 1 slice ham
- 3 semi-dried (sun-blushed) tomatoes, chopped
- 2 teaspoons capers, chopped
- 1–2 slices cheddar cheese

Preheat grill (broiler). Cut the bread in half horizontally and grill both slices. To make the aïoli, mix a little crushed garlic into the mayonnaise and season well with salt and pepper.

Spread the aïoli over the insides of both halves. Place ham, semi-dried tomatoes and capers on the base piece. Top with cheese slices to make a generous layer and place on a baking tray.

Grill the sandwich until the cheese has melted and is starting to bubble. Put the top back on; press down firmly.

Serves 1

Steak sandwich with salsa verde

1 small garlic clove, crushed
1 large handful parsley
1 handful basil leaves
1 handful mint leaves
1 tablespoon olive oil
1 teaspoon capers, chopped
1 teaspoon lemon juice
1 teaspoon red wine vinegar
1 teaspoon olive oil, extra
1 minute steak – about 80 g (3 oz)
1 large piece ciabatta or Turkish bread, halved horizontally
¼ Lebanese (short) cucumber, sliced

To make salsa verde, put the garlic, herbs and oil in a food processor and whizz them together until coarsely chopped. Place the mixture in a bowl and stir in the capers, lemon juice and vinegar. Season with salt and pepper.

Heat extra oil in a small frying pan (skillet) and fry steak for 1 minute on each side — it will cook very quickly and start to brown.

While steak is cooking, toast bread. Spread the salsa verde on the bread base and make a sandwich with the steak and cucumber.

Serves 1

Pizzette

75 g (2¼ oz/½ cup) plain (all-purpose) flour
75 g (2¼ oz/½ cup) wholemeal (whole-wheat) plain (all-purpose) flour
1 teaspoon dry yeast
¼ teaspoon sugar
¼ teaspoon salt
1 tablespoon plain yoghurt
1 tablespoon tomato paste (purée)
1 small garlic clove, crushed
½ teaspoon dried oregano
2-3 slices lean shaved ham, chopped
2 tablespoons grated mozzarella cheese
chopped rocket (arugula), to serve
extra virgin olive oil, to serve

Note: Freeze the other uncooked pizzette for another day. Defrost it and return it to room temperature before cooking. If preferred, you can purchase ready-made pizza bases or use Lebanese bread as a base.

Sift plain flour into a bowl, then add the wholemeal plain flour, dry yeast, sugar and salt. Make a well in the centre, add 60 ml (2 fl oz/¼ cup) water and yoghurt and mix to a dough. Knead on a lightly floured surface for 5 minutes, or until smooth and elastic. Cover with a tea (dish) towel and rest in a warm place for 20–30 minutes, or until doubled in size.

Preheat oven to 200°C (400°F/Gas 6). Punch the dough down and knead for 30 seconds, then divide it into two portions. Roll each portion into a 15 cm (6 inch) round. Place on a baking tray.

Combine the tomato paste, garlic, oregano and 2 teaspoons water and spread over each base. Top with the ham and mozzarella.

For a single serve, bake one of the pizzettes for 12–15 minutes, or until crisp and golden on edges. Just before serving, top with the chopped rocket and drizzle with extra virgin olive oil.

Makes 2

Salade niçoise

2 small salad potatoes (150 g/6 oz), peeled
50 g (2 oz) small green beans, topped, tailed and halved
1 teaspoon olive oil
100 g (3½ oz) tuna steak, cubed

Dressing
1 small garlic clove, crushed
½ teaspoon dijon mustard
1 tablespoon white wine vinegar
60 ml (2 fl oz/¼ cup) olive oil, extra

1 handful green lettuce leaves
4 cherry tomatoes, halved
6 black olives
2 teaspoons capers, drained
1 hard-boiled egg, cut into wedges
2 anchovies, halved
lemon wedges

Note: Store any leftover dressing in a jar and refrigerate.

Cook the potatoes in boiling salted water for about 10 minutes, or until they are just tender. Drain, cut into wedges, then place in a bowl. Cook the beans in boiling salted water for 3 minutes, then drain and hold under cold running water for a minute (this will stop them cooking any further). Add them to the potatoes.

Heat olive oil in a small frying pan (skillet) and, when it is hot, cook the tuna cubes for about 3 minutes, or until browned on all sides. Add these cubes to the potatoes and beans.

To make dressing, whisk together the garlic, mustard and vinegar in a small bowl, then add the extra oil in a thin, steady stream, whisking until smooth. Season well.

Cover the base of a serving bowl or plate with the lettuce leaves. Scatter the potatoes, beans, tuna, tomatoes, olives and capers over the leaves and drizzle with some of the dressing. Add the egg wedges and anchovies and a squeeze of lemon juice.

Serves 1

Bacon and avocado salad

2 bacon slices, rinds cut off
80 g (3 oz) green beans, topped, tailed and halved
80 g (3 oz) baby spinach leaves
1 French shallot, finely sliced
1 small avocado

Dressing
¼ teaspoon brown sugar
1 small garlic clove, crushed
2 tablespoons olive oil
3 teaspoons balsamic vinegar
½ teaspoon sesame oil

Preheat grill (broiler). Put the bacon on a tray and grill on both sides until it is nice and crisp. Leave it to cool and then break into pieces.

Bring a saucepan of water to the boil and cook the beans for 4 minutes. Drain and then hold them under cold running water for a few seconds to stop them cooking any further.

Put spinach in a deep serving bowl and add beans, bacon and shallots. Halve the avocado, cut it into cubes and add to the salad.

To make the dressing, mix brown sugar and garlic in a small bowl. Add the remaining ingredients and whisk together well. Drizzle some of the dressing over the salad and toss well to coat. Add a grinding of black pepper and a sprinkling of salt.

Note: Store any leftover dressing in a screwtop jar and refrigerate.

Serves 1

Goat's cheese, leek and tapenade parcel

40 g (1½ oz) butter
1 leek, thinly sliced
2 sheets filo pastry
2 teaspoons tapenade
1 small thyme sprig
1 small round of goat's cheese or
 1 thick slice from a log of cheese

Preheat the oven to 180°C (350°F/ Gas 4). Melt half the butter in a pan, add the leek and stir until coated in butter. Cook slowly over a low heat until tender.

Melt the rest of the butter in a small saucepan. Place one sheet of filo on the work surface with the short end facing you. Brush pastry with butter. Lay the other sheet on top of it and cover with a tea (dish) towel (dish towel) to stop the pastry drying out.

When the leek is cooked and cooled, spread the tapenade over the middle of the pastry sheet, leaving a wide border around the edges. Spread the leek over the tapenade. Top with the goat's cheese and then a thyme sprig. Fold the bottom part of pastry up and the two sides in, to enclose the filling, then fold the top end down and roll the whole parcel over.

Brush the pastry with butter. Bake the parcel for 20 minutes. Pastry should be browned and the filling melted.

Serves 1

Spinach salad with chicken and sesame dressing

80 g (3 oz) baby spinach leaves
½ Lebanese (short) cucumber, peeled and diced
1 spring onion (scallion), shredded
1 small carrot, cut into matchsticks
1 small cooked chicken breast
1 tablespoon tahini
1 tablespoon lime juice
1½ teaspoons sesame oil
½ teaspoon sugar
pinch of chilli flakes
2 teaspoons sesame seeds
a small handful coriander (cilantro) leaves

Put the spinach in a large serving bowl. Scatter the cucumber, spring onion and carrot over the top. Shred the chicken breast into long pieces and scatter it over the vegetables.

Combine the tahini, lime juice, sesame oil, sugar and chilli flakes. Add salt to taste. Drizzle dressing over the salad.

Cook sesame seeds in a dry frying pan (skillet) over a low heat for about 1 minute, stirring them around. When they start to brown and smell toasted, tip them over salad. Scatter coriander on top. Toss salad just before serving.

Serves 1

Chicken sandwich

2 teaspoons olive oil
3 chicken tenderloins
2 teaspoons lemon juice
1 large piece ciabatta or Turkish bread, cut in half horizontally
1 garlic clove, peeled and cut in half
mayonnaise
½ avocado, sliced
1 tomato, sliced
a handful of rocket (arugula) leaves, long stems snapped off

Heat oil in a small frying pan (skillet), add chicken tenderloins and fry on both sides for a couple of minutes, or until brown and cooked through. Sprinkle with lemon juice, then remove chicken from pan. Add bread to pan, cut-side-down, and cook for 1 minute, pressing down on it to flatten it and to help soak up any juices.

Take bread out of pan, rub the cut side of the garlic over the surface, then spread both pieces with a generous amount of mayonnaise. Place chicken tenderloins on the bread base, season and layer with avocado and tomato, seasoning as you go. Finish with the rocket and the top of the bread.

Serves 1

Vietnamese chicken salad

1 small cooked chicken breast or 2 boneless cooked chicken thighs
1 tablespoon lime juice
3 teaspoons fish sauce
pinch sugar
¼ bird's eye chilli, finely chopped
1 small garlic clove, crushed
1 French shallot, finely sliced
1 large handful bean sprouts
1 large handful shredded Chinese cabbage
1 tablespoon finely chopped Vietnamese mint or mint leaves

Shred the cooked chicken and put it in a deep serving bowl.

Combine lime juice, fish sauce, sugar, chilli, garlic and shallot in a small bowl.

Bring a saucepan of water to the boil; add bean sprouts. After 10 seconds, drain and rinse under cold water to stop them cooking further.

Add bean sprouts, Chinese cabbage and Vietnamese mint to the chicken. Pour the dressing over the salad and toss well to combine.

Serves 1

Barbecued honey chicken wings

6 chicken wings
2 tablespoons soy sauce
1½ tablespoons sherry
1½ tablespoons oil
1 small garlic clove, crushed
1½ tablespoons honey

Rinse the chicken wings, then pat dry with paper towels. Tuck the wing tips into the underside.

Put chicken in a shallow non-metallic dish. In a small bowl, whisk the soy sauce, sherry, oil and garlic, then pour mixture over chicken and lightly toss. Cover with plastic wrap and refrigerate for 2 hours to marinate, turning the wings occasionally.

The honey needs to be heated enough for it to become brushing consistency — either use the microwave or warm it gently in a small saucepan.

Lightly grease a barbecue or chargrill pan (griddle) and heat it. Lift chicken out of the marinade and place in the hot pan. Cook until tender and cooked through, turning occasionally — this should take about 12 minutes. Brush with the warmed honey and cook for a further 2 minutes.

Serves 1

Bean enchiladas

2 teaspoons light olive oil
½ small onion, finely sliced
2 garlic cloves, crushed
⅛ bird's eye chilli, seeded and finely chopped
1 teaspoon ground cumin
60 ml (2 fl oz/¼ cup) vegetable stock or water
1 large tomato, peeled, seeded and chopped
2 teaspoons tomato paste (purée)
300 g (10½ oz) tin three-bean mix
1 tablespoon chopped coriander (cilantro) leaves
2 flour tortillas
½ small avocado, peeled and chopped
2 tablespoons light sour cream
few coriander (cilantro) sprigs
a handful of shredded lettuce

Heat oil in a deep frying pan (skillet) over medium heat. Add the onion and cook for 3–4 minutes, or until just soft. Add garlic and chilli and cook for a further 30 seconds. Add the cumin, vegetable stock, tomato and tomato paste; cook for 6–8 minutes, or until the mixture is quite thick and pulpy. Season with salt and freshly ground black pepper.

Preheat the oven to 170°C (325°F/ Gas 3). Drain and rinse beans, add to the sauce and cook 5 minutes to heat through. Add chopped coriander.

Meanwhile, wrap tortillas in cooking foil and warm in oven for 3–4 minutes.

To assemble, place one tortilla on a plate and spread with half of the bean mixture. Top with half of the avocado, sour cream, coriander sprigs and the lettuce. Roll the enchilada up, tucking in the ends. Repeat with the other tortilla. Cut each one in half to serve.

Serves 1

Steamed rice noodle rolls

175 g (6 oz) barbecued or roast duck
2 rice noodle rolls
1 spring onion (scallion), finely shredded
1 thick slice fresh ginger, finely shredded
a small handful coriander (cilantro) leaves
oyster sauce, for drizzling
chilli sauce, to serve

Note: Barbecued chicken can be used instead of duck. Rice noodle rolls and barbecued duck are available from Asian stores.

Cut the duck into bite-sized pieces. You may have to strip the flesh off the bones first, depending on how you bought it — leave the skin on but trim off any fatty bits.

Gently unroll the noodle rolls. If they are a bit stiff, steam or microwave them for a minute or two. If they are in a vacuum-wrapped package, you can drop the wrapped package in boiling water for 5 minutes.

Put half of the duck at one edge of the narrower end of one noodle roll and arrange some spring onion, ginger and coriander over it. Drizzle with little oyster sauce and roll up the sheet. Repeat this with the remaining sheets. Put the sheets on a heatproof plate.

Put the plate in a bamboo or metal steamer and set steamer over a pan filled with simmering water. Steam, covered, for 5 minutes. Serve rolls cut into lengths with oyster sauce drizzled over them and chilli sauce on the side.

Serves 1

Prawn mango salad

Dressing
1 tablespoon sour cream
60 ml (2 fl oz/¼ cup) mango purée (*see* Note)
1 tablespoon lime juice
1 teaspoon sweet chilli sauce

1 slice of bacon, rind removed, chopped
4-6 cooked king prawns (shrimp), peeled and deveined, with tails intact
1 small mango, peeled and cut into thin wedges
1 small avocado, sliced

Note: Use mango purée from a can or mash a fresh mango cheek to get 60 ml (2 fl oz/¼ cup) purée.

To make the dressing, combine all the ingredients in a small bowl and whisk until smooth.

Cook bacon in a frying pan (skillet) until crisp. Drain on paper towels.

Arrange prawns, mango and avocado on a serving plate and sprinkle with bacon bits. Drizzle with the dressing.

Serves 1

Spiced parsnip and bacon cake

2 parsnips, peeled and sliced
1 tablespoon butter
2 slices of bacon, rind removed, chopped
¼—½ small red chilli, seeded and finely chopped
1 French shallot, finely chopped
½ teaspoon garam masala

1 tablespoon wholegrain mustard
2 teaspoons honey
60 ml (2 fl oz/¼ cup) cream
green salad leaves, to serve

Bring a saucepan of water to the boil and cook the parsnips at a simmer for 15 minutes. Drain them well.

Melt half the butter in a small non-stick frying pan (skillet), add bacon and cook until browned. Add chilli and chopped shallot and cook for 2 minutes. Stir in garam masala; remove from the heat.

Mash the parsnips in a bowl, then mix in the bacon mixture. Return pan to the heat with remaining butter. Pile parsnip mixture into the pan and flatten it with a spatula. Cook for a few minutes — it should hold together in a cake. Loosen the cake, slide it out onto a plate, then invert the plate back over the frying pan and flip the cake back in to cook the other side.

While cake is cooking, heat mustard, honey and cream in a small pan over low heat until the mixture bubbles.

When both sides of cake are brown, turn it out onto a board and slice it into wedges. Serve with honey and mustard sauce and the salad leaves.

Serves 1

Crisp lavash with mixed mushrooms

1 piece lavash or Lebanese bread
1 tablespoon olive oil
1 tablespoon finely grated parmesan cheese
30 g (1 oz) butter
1 spring onion (scallion), sliced
185 g (6½ oz) mixed mushrooms (field, button, swiss browns, pine, enoki), sliced
chervil leaves, to garnish

Preheat oven to 180°C (350°F/Gas 4). Cut lavash into 2.5 cm (1 inch) wide strips, brush lightly with a little oil and sprinkle with parmesan cheese. Bake for 10 minutes, or until crisp.

Heat the butter and the remaining oil in a medium frying pan (skillet) until sizzling. Add the spring onion and the field mushrooms and cook over a medium heat until the mushrooms are tender. Add button, swiss brown and pine mushrooms and cook until the liquid has evaporated. Remove from heat and stir through the enoki mushrooms.

Arrange the lavash in an interlocking square on a serving plate. Pile the mushrooms in the centre and garnish with chervil.

Serves 1

Goat's cheese and pear toasts

4 slices bread from a breadstick
quince paste, for spreading
1 corella pear, quartered and cored
50 g (1¾ oz) log goat's cheese
extra virgin olive oil, to serve

Note: If corella pears are not available, just use any smallish pear.

Preheat the grill (broiler) to high. Place bread slices on the grill tray and toast under the hot grill for a few minutes on both sides, until lightly golden. Cool, then spread with some quince paste.

Cut the pear quarters lengthways into thin slices and arrange on each slice of toast. Arrange the goat's cheese (don't worry if it crumbles a little) on top of the pear slices.

Cook the toasts under the hot grill for about 1 minute to warm and soften cheese — it won't melt completely. Drizzle with the extra virgin olive oil, season with cracked black pepper and serve hot.

Makes 4 slices

Chunky parmesan toasts

1 tablespoon butter, softened
2 tablespoons finely grated parmesan cheese
2 teaspoons finely snipped chives
2 thick slices of white sandwich bread

Note: You can vary this recipe by adding garlic or even a little chilli to the butter. Alternatively, use finely chopped basil along with the chives for a wonderfully fresh herb flavour.

Heat the grill (broiler) to high. Combine butter, cheese and chives in a small bowl and mix well.

Spread each slice of bread with butter mixture and arrange on the grill tray. Cook for about 1–2 minutes, or until tops are lightly golden. Slice toasts in half and serve while crisp and hot.

Makes 2

Semolina with three cheeses

125 ml (4 fl oz/½ cup) chicken stock
185 ml (6 fl oz/¾ cup) milk
60 g (2¼ oz/½ cup) fine semolina
1 egg yolk
2 tablespoons finely grated parmesan cheese
3 tablespoons finely chopped parsley
30 g (1 oz) mild gorgonzola cheese, crumbled
30 g (1oz/¼ cup) coarsely grated cheddar cheese
2 tablespoons thick (double/heavy) cream

Note: Cover the remaining prepared dish with plastic wrap and refrigerate. The next day, reheat under the grill for 8 minutes or until hot and bubbling. This dish is not suitable for freezing.

Pour stock and milk into a large pan. Bring to the boil, then remove from heat. Add the semolina in a slow, steady stream, whisking constantly to prevent lumps forming. Put pan back over medium heat and whisk for 3 minutes, or until mixture has boiled and is very thick. Turn off the heat. Working quickly and using a wooden spoon, beat in the egg yolk, parmesan and the parsley and season to taste. Spread mixture into two lightly oiled, shallow, 250 ml (9 fl oz/1 cup) square or round baking dishes. Stand at room temperature for 1 hour, or until firm.

Heat grill (broiler) to medium. Turn semolina out onto a board (keep baking dishes handy). With a wet knife, cut semolina into four squares; place on a lightly oiled baking tray.

Grill for 4—5 minutes on each side, or until well browned. Turn the grill up high. Arrange and fit the semolina pieces, slightly overlapping, back in the baking dishes. Sprinkle evenly with the gorgonzola and cheddar and drizzle with cream. For one serve, put a baking dish under the grill and cook for 5 minutes, or until cheese is hot and bubbling. Serve warm, sprinkled with a cracked black pepper.

Makes 2

Grilled cheesy club sandwich

1 slice bacon, halved
1½ tablespoons mayonnaise
1 small garlic clove, crushed
1 teaspoon lemon juice
3 thin, large slices country-style or sourdough bread
1 small tomato, sliced
2 thin slices swiss or jarlsberg cheese
½ small ripe avocado, coarsely mashed

Heat grill (broiler) to high. Put the bacon on the grill tray and grill for 2 minutes on each side, or until lightly browned but not crisp.

Combine the mayonnaise, garlic and lemon juice in a small bowl and season well with freshly ground black pepper.

Put 2 bread slices under the grill and toast on one side for about 1 minute, or until golden. Place a slice on a work surface, toasted-side-down. Spread with half the garlic mayonnaise, add tomato slices, then a slice of cheese. Put the untoasted slice of bread on top, spread with the remaining garlic mayonnaise and sit the bacon on top.

Pile on the avocado, then top with the remaining slice of grilled bread, placing it toasted-side-up. Press the sandwich down firmly. Place remaining slice of cheese on top of sandwich, allowing the cheese to fall over the sides a little.

Return the sandwich to the grill and cook for 1 minute, or until the cheese bubbles and browns. Cool slightly, then cut in half diagonally. Serve warm.

Serves 1

Carrot and almond salad

2 large carrots, peeled
1 tablespoon peanut oil
½ teaspoon caster (superfine) sugar
¼ teaspoon brown mustard seeds
⅛ teaspoon curry powder
1 tablespoon lemon juice
1 tablespoon toasted flaked almonds
1 small handful coriander (cilantro) leaves
thick plain yoghurt, to serve

Note: Serve this as a side dish with barbecued or grilled chicken. Cover and refrigerate leftover salad (without the yoghurt) for up to 3 days.

Heat grill (broiler) to medium. Slice carrots thinly, on the diagonal. Put half of the oil in a bowl, mix in sugar, then add carrot and toss to coat. Spread the carrot on a baking tray and grill for 10–15 minutes, turning occasionally, until lightly browned and tender. Remove from heat and leave to cool. Place in a bowl.

While carrots are grilling, heat the remaining oil in a small frying pan (skillet). Add mustard seeds and curry powder and cook over low heat for 1 minute, or until fragrant.

Allow to cool a little, then whisk in lemon juice and season well. Drizzle spice mixture over the carrots, add almonds and coriander and toss gently until combined. Serve at room temperature, with a dollop of yoghurt.

Serves 1

Smoked mozzarella sandwich

2 thick slices ciabatta or other Italian-style bread
butter, for spreading
3 thin slices smoked mozzarella cheese
1 small vine-ripened tomatoes, thinly sliced
2 large basil leaves

Note: Look for smoked mozzarella cheese at delicatessens or speciality cheese stores.

Preheat a barbecue flat plate or a grill plate to medium. Spread the slices of bread with the butter, then place 1slice, buttered-side-down, on a work surface. Layer the cheese, tomato and basil on top, then add the other bread slice, placing it buttered-side-up. Tie sandwich together with kitchen string.

Put sandwich on hotplate, pressing it down firmly with a spatula. Grill for 3 minutes, pressing down firmly during cooking. Turn and cook for another 2 minutes, pressing down firmly with the spatula again, until the bread is golden brown and filling has heated through.

Remove from the heat, discard string and cut the sandwich crossways into three 'fingers'. Arrange on a serving plate and serve sprinkled with sea salt.

Serves 1

Every night

Baked chicken and leek risotto

1 tablespoon butter
½ small leek, thinly sliced
1 boneless, skinless chicken breast fillet, cut into small cubes
110 g (3¾ oz/½ cup) arborio rice
1 tablespoon white wine
310 ml (11 fl oz/1¼ cups) chicken stock
1 tablespoon grated parmesan cheese
2 teaspoons thyme leaves, plus extra to garnish
freshly grated parmesan cheese, extra

Note: Leftover risotto will keep, covered and refrigerated, for up to 2 days. Reheat in the microwave.

Preheat the oven to 150°C (300°F/Gas 2). Put a 1 litre (35 fl oz/4 cups) ovenproof dish with a lid in the oven.

Heat the butter in a saucepan over medium heat, stir in the leek and cook for about 2 minutes, then add the chicken and stir for 3 minutes. Toss in the rice and stir for 1 minute. Add the wine and stock, and bring to the boil.

Pour into the dish and cover. Cook in the oven for 20—25 minutes, stirring halfway through. Remove from the oven and stir in cheese and thyme. Season. Pile into a serving bowl and sprinkle with extra thyme and cheese.

Serves 1

Spaghetti carbonara

2 teaspoons olive oil
85 g (3 oz) pancetta, cut into small dice
60 ml (2 fl oz/¼ cup) thick (double/heavy) cream
2 egg yolks
100 g (3½ oz) spaghetti
2 tablespoons grated parmesan cheese

Heat olive oil in a small frying pan (skillet) and cook the pancetta, stirring frequently, until light brown and crisp.

Mix the cream and egg yolks together in a bowl, and when the pancetta has cooled, add it to the egg mixture.

Cook spaghetti in a large saucepan of boiling salted water until al dente, stirring once or twice to make sure the pieces are not stuck together. Drain the spaghetti and reserve a quarter cup of the cooking water.

Put spaghetti back in the saucepan and put it over a low heat. Add the egg mixture and half the parmesan, then take pan off the heat, otherwise the egg will scramble. Season with salt and pepper and mix together. If sauce is too thick and pasta is stuck together, add a little of the reserved cooking water. The spaghetti should look as if it has a fine coating of egg and cream all over it.

Serve spaghetti in a warm bowl with parmesan sprinkled over the top.

Serves 1

Minestrone alla milanese

65 g (2¼ oz/⅓ cup) dried borlotti beans
1 tablespoon butter
1 small onion, finely chopped
1 garlic clove, finely chopped
1 tablespoon finely chopped parsley
1 sage leaf
40 g (1½ oz) pancetta, cubed
1 small celery stalk, halved, then sliced
1 small carrot, sliced
1 potato, peeled but left whole
1 teaspoon tomato paste (purée)
200 g (7 oz) tinned chopped tomatoes
4 basil leaves
1 litre (35 fl oz/4 cups) chicken or vegetable stock
1 small zucchini (courgette), sliced
40 g (1½ oz/¼ cup) fresh or frozen peas
6 runner beans, cut into 4 cm (1½ inch) lengths
a handful shredded cabbage
55 g (2 oz/¼ cup) arborio rice
grated parmesan cheese, to serve

Note: Freeze in serving size containers and defrost as needed. Instead of soaking dried borlotti beans you can add a 300 g tin of drained beans at the end of cooking and reduce the initial cooking time by 1 hour.

Put dried beans in a large bowl, cover with cold water and soak overnight. Drain and rinse under cold water.

Melt the butter in a saucepan and add the onion, garlic, parsley, sage and pancetta. Cook over low heat, stirring until the onion is soft. Add celery, carrot and potato, and cook for 5 minutes. Stir in tomato paste, tomatoes, basil and borlotti beans. Season with pepper. Add stock and bring slowly to the boil. Cover and leave to simmer for 2 hours, stirring once or twice. Add a little more stock or water if needed.

If the potato has not broken up, roughly break with a fork against the side of the pan. Taste for seasoning and add the zucchini, peas, runner beans, cabbage and the rice. Simmer until the rice is cooked. Ladle a single portion into a deep bowl and sprinkle over some parmesan cheese.

Makes about 7 cups/portions

Tuna mornay

30 g (1 oz) butter
1 tablespoon plain (all-purpose) flour
250 ml (9 fl oz/1 cup) milk
¼ teaspoon dry mustard
40 g (1½ oz/⅓ cup) grated cheddar cheese
300 g (10½ oz) tinned tuna in brine, drained
1 tablespoon finely chopped parsley
1 egg, hard-boiled and chopped
2 tablespoons fresh or dried breadcrumbs
paprika, for dusting

Preheat oven to 180°C (350°F/Gas 4). Melt butter in a small saucepan, add the flour and stir over low heat for 1 minute. Take pan off the heat and slowly pour in milk, stirring with your other hand until you have a smooth sauce. Return pan to the heat and stir constantly until sauce boils and thickens. Reduce heat and simmer for another 2 minutes. Remove pan from heat, whisk in mustard and two-thirds of the cheese — don't stop whisking until you have a smooth, rich cheesy sauce.

Roughly flake tuna with a fork, then tip it into the cheesy sauce, along with the parsley and egg. Season with a little salt and pepper, then spoon the mixture into two 250 ml (9 fl oz/1 cup) ovenproof ramekins.

Make topping by mixing breadcrumbs and remaining cheese together, then sprinkle it over the mornay. Add a little colour by dusting the top very lightly with paprika.

For one serving, place one dish on a small tray in the oven and cook for about 15 minutes until the topping is golden brown.

Makes 2 serves/portions

Note: Cover and refrigerate the remaining prepared dish. Cook the next day as needed.

Eggplant parmigiana

375 g (13 oz) eggplant (aubergine)
plain (all-purpose) flour, seasoned with salt and pepper
olive oil, for frying
250 ml (9 fl oz/1 cup) tomato passata or tomato pasta sauce
2 tablespoons roughly torn basil leaves
75 g (2½ oz/½ cup) mozzarella cheese, chopped
35 g (1¼ oz/⅓ cup) grated parmesan cheese

Note: Cool the remaining parmigiana, then cover with foil and refrigerate. Reheat next day in a 180°C (350°F/Gas 4) oven for 20 minutes.To reduce amount of oil used you can brush the unfloured slices with oil and grill for 5 minutes, turning once, until tender.

Thinly slice eggplant into about nine 1 cm slices. Layer the slices in a large colander, sprinkling salt between each layer. Leave for 1 hour to degorge. Rinse and pat slices dry on both sides with paper towels, then coat lightly with the flour.

Preheat oven to 180°C (350°F/Gas 4) and grease a shallow 1 litre (35 fl oz/4 cups) baking dish.

Heat about 60 ml (2 fl oz/¼ cup) of olive oil in a large frying pan (skillet). Quickly fry eggplant slices in batches over high heat until crisp and golden on both sides. Add more olive oil as needed and drain on paper towels as you remove each batch from the pan.

Make a slightly overlapping layer of eggplant slices over the base of the dish. Season with pepper and a little salt. Spoon a third of passata over the eggplant and scatter some basil over top. Sprinkle with mozzarella, followed by some parmesan. Continue layering until all the ingredients are used up, finishing with a layer of the cheeses.

Bake for 25-30 minutes. Remove from oven and allow to cool for 15 minutes before cutting a single serve slice.

Serves 1

Pizza margherita

1 ready-made pizza base or Lebanese bread
2 very ripe roma (plum) tomatoes
about 10 basil leaves
1 garlic clove, crushed
1 tablespoon tomato passata or tomato pasta sauce
about 1 tablespoon olive oil
100 g (3½ oz/⅔ cup) fresh mozzarella cheese, chopped

Heat the oven to as high as it will go — the pizza should cook as quickly as possible.

Remove cores, seeds and juices from the tomatoes, chop tomatoes roughly, then purée them in a food processor with 4 of the basil leaves. Stir in garlic, passata and 1 teaspoon of the olive oil and season well.

Put base on an oiled tray. Drizzle with a little of the olive oil. Spoon tomato sauce over the base, spreading it up to the rim. Scatter the mozzarella over the top and drizzle with a little more olive oil.

Cook pizza for 5–12 minutes (this will depend on how hot your oven is), or until base is light brown and crisp and topping is cooked. Before serving, drizzle with a little more oil and scatter remaining basil over the top.

Makes 1 pizza

Mushroom soup

- 1 tablespoon butter
- 1 small onion, finely chopped
- 4 large (about 200 g/7 oz) field mushrooms, finely chopped
- 1 garlic clove, crushed
- 1 tablespoon dry sherry
- about 125 ml (4 fl oz/½ cup) chicken or vegetable stock
- 1 tablespoon finely chopped parsley
- 1 tablespoon cream

Note: Leftover soup can be refrigerated for up to 2 days. Gently reheat before serving.

Melt butter in a saucepan and fry the onion until the onion is translucent but not browned. Add the mushroom and garlic and continue frying. Initially the mushrooms might give off some liquid, so keep frying until it is all absorbed back into the mixture. This will take 8—10 minutes.

Add sherry to pan, turn up the heat and let mixture bubble — this burns off the alcohol but leaves the flavour. Cool slightly, then transfer to a blender (or use an immersion blender). Whizz together until a smooth paste forms, then add enough stock to create the desired consistency and blend until smooth. Add the parsley and cream and blend together. Pour back into the saucepan and heat gently. Serve with bread.

Serves 1

Prawns with garlic and chilli

2 tablespoons olive oil
2 garlic cloves, crushed
½ small red onion, finely chopped
1 dried chilli, cut in half, seeds removed
6–8 large prawns (shrimp), peeled and deveined, tails left intact
1 large tomato, peeled and finely chopped
1 tablespoon chopped parsley or coriander (cilantro)
bread, to serve

Heat the oil in a small frying pan (skillet) or shallow casserole dish. Add garlic, onion and chilli, cook for a few minutes, then add the prawns and cook them for about 4 minutes, by which time they should be pink all over.

When the prawns are cooked, add tomato and cook for a minute or two. Season with salt and stir the herbs through. Take pan to the table, and put it on a heatproof mat. Eat with bread to mop up the juices.

Serves 1

Imam bayildi

1 eggplant (aubergine)
2½ tablespoons olive oil
1 onion, chopped
1 garlic clove, crushed
3 ripe tomatoes, chopped
½ teaspoon ground cinnamon
a small handful parsley, chopped
250 ml (9 fl oz/1 cup) tomato juice
thick plain yoghurt

Preheat oven to 200°C (400°F/Gas 6). Cut the eggplant in half lengthways. To hollow out the middle, run a small sharp knife around the edge of each cut half, about 1 cm (½ inch) from the skin. Dig out the flesh in the middle, within the cut line, to leave two shells. Keep the flesh and chop it finely.

Heat 2 tablespoons of oil in a frying pan (skillet) and fry the eggplant flesh, onion and garlic until the onion is soft and cooked through. Add tomato and any juices and stir everything together. Season with salt and pepper and add the cinnamon. Cook the mixture until it is dryish, then stir in the parsley.

Fill eggplant shells with the mixture and put them in a baking dish. Pour the tomato juice around the eggplant — this will help stop eggplant drying out as it cooks. Drizzle with a little extra olive oil.

Bake the eggplant shells for 1 hour, by which time the flesh should be tender and the filling brown on top. Serve one half with some of the tomato juice spooned over and a dollop of yoghurt on top.

Makes 2 serves/portions

Note: Cover and refrigerate the remaining half; it can be eaten cold the next day. If preferred, it can be reheated on a baking tray in a 200°C (400°F/Gas 6) oven for 20 minutes.

Sausages cooked with lentils

1 tablespoon olive oil
2—4 Italian sausages
1 small onion, chopped
2 garlic cloves, thinly sliced
1 tablespoon finely chopped rosemary
400 g (14 oz) tin chopped tomatoes
8 juniper berries, lightly crushed
½ teaspoon freshly grated nutmeg
1 bay leaf
small pinch dried chilli flakes
100 ml (3½ fl oz) red wine
45 g (1½ oz/¼ cup) green lentils
extra rosemary, to garnish

Note: Cover and refrigerate leftover lentils and sausages. Gently reheat the next day. You can also freeze a portion in an airtight container for up to 1 month.

Heat the olive oil in a saucepan and cook the sausages for 5–10 minutes, browning well all over. Remove the sausages and set aside.

Reduce heat to low, add the onion and garlic to the pan and cook until the onion is soft and translucent, but not browned. Stir in rosemary, then add tomatoes and cook gently until the sauce has thickened.

Add the juniper berries, nutmeg, bay leaf, chilli, red wine and 200 ml (7 fl oz) water. Bring to the boil, then add the lentils and the cooked sausages. Stir well, cover the saucepan and simmer gently for about 40 minutes, or until the lentils are soft. Stir the lentils a few times to prevent them sticking to the base of the pan and add a little more water if you need to cook them for a bit longer. Remove the bay leaf and chilli before serving. For 1 serve pile a portion onto a plate and top with 1 or 2 sausages. Garnish with rosemary.

Makes 2 serves/portions

Rice noodles with beef, black beans and capsicums

85 g (3oz) rump steak
1 garlic clove, crushed
1½ tablespoons oyster sauce
1 teaspoon sugar
1 tablespoon soy sauce
2 tablespoons black bean sauce
1 teaspoon cornflour (cornstarch)
½ teaspoon sesame oil
250 g (9 oz) fresh or 125 g (4½ oz) dried flat rice noodles
1 tablespoon oil
1 small red capsicum (pepper), sliced
½ small green capsicum (pepper), sliced
a small handful coriander (cilantro) leaves

Cut steak across the grain into thin slices and put it in a bowl with the garlic, oyster sauce, sugar, soy sauce, black bean sauce, cornflour and the sesame oil. Mix everything together, making sure slices are all well coated.

If you are using dried rice noodles, soak them in boiling water for about 10 minutes, or until they are opaque and soft. If the noodles are particularly dry, they may need a little longer. Drain noodles.

Heat the oil in a wok or frying pan (skillet) and, when it is hot, add the capsicums. Stir-fry the capsicums for a minute or two until they are starting to soften, then add meat mixture and cook for a minute. Add noodles and toss everything together well. Keep cooking until beef is cooked through and everything is hot, then toss in the coriander leaves and stir once before turning off heat. Serve straight away.

Serves 1

Cheesy bubble and squeak cakes with bacon

- 1 large or 2 small floury potatoes, peeled
- 2 teaspoons milk
- 2 teaspoons butter
- 75 g (2½ oz/1 cup) thinly shredded savoy cabbage
- 30 g (1 oz/¼ cup) cheddar cheese, grated
- 1 tablespoon oil, for frying
- 2 bacon slices, rinds cut off

Cut the potatoes into pieces and cook them in a small saucepan of simmering water for 10 minutes, or until soft. Drain well, put them back in the pan with the milk and mash until smooth. Season with salt and pepper.

Melt butter in a non-stick frying pan (skillet) and cook the cabbage until it is soft. Add this to the potato along with the cheese. The mixture should be stiff enough to form the potato into cakes — it is up to you whether you make 1 large or 2 smaller ones.

Heat oil in the same frying pan (skillet) over a medium heat and cook bacon on both sides until it is crisp. Remove the bacon from the pan, keep warm. Add the potato cakes to the pan and fry on both sides until they are well browned and slightly crisp. Shake pan occasionally to move cakes around so they don't stick. Serve with the bacon.

Serves 1

Saffron fish cakes with herb crème fraîche

80 ml (2½ fl oz/⅓ cup) milk
1 pinch saffron threads
250 g (9 oz) (about 2 medium fillets) boneless white fish fillets
2 large potatoes, peeled and cut into chunks
1 garlic clove, unpeeled
1 tablespoon plain (all-purpose) flour
1 teaspoon grated lemon zest
a small handful parsley, finely chopped
1 tablespoon cream
2 tablespoons crème fraîche
1 tablespoon finely chopped mint
1 tablespoon finely chopped parsley
1–2 tablespoons butter

Note: Any leftover fish cakes can be reheated gently in a 150°C (300°F/Gas 3) oven for 10 minutes or can be microwaved. They will keep, covered and refrigerated, for 1 day.

Put the milk and saffron in a frying pan (skillet) and heat until simmering. Add the fish, turn up the heat a little and cook until the fish turns opaque and flaky — you might need to turn it over halfway through. Don't worry if it breaks up. Lift the fish out of the milk into a bowl and break it up roughly with a fork. Keep the milk.

Cook the potato and the garlic clove in simmering water for 12 minutes, or until potato is tender. Drain the potato and put it back in the saucepan. Peel garlic and add it to the potato, mash everything together and strain in the saffron milk. Keep mashing until the mixture is smooth, then stir in the fish, flour, half the lemon zest, parsley and cream. Season well.

Shape mixture into three or four even-sized cakes. Put in the fridge to chill while you make the herb crème fraîche by mixing together the crème fraîche, remaining lemon zest and herbs.

Heat butter in a large non-stick frying pan (skillet) and cook fish cakes for 3 minutes on each side — they should have a brown crust. Serve with the crème fraîche.

Serves 1

Stir-fried chicken with ginger and cashews

1 tablespoon oil
2—3 spring onions (scallions), cut into pieces
2 garlic cloves, crushed
3 cm (1¼ inch) piece ginger, finely shredded
1 small skinless chicken breast, cut into strips
1 small red capsicum (pepper), cut into strips
50 g (1¾ oz) snow peas (mangetout)
40 g (1½ oz/¼ cup) cashews
1 tablespoon soy sauce
½ teaspoon sesame oil

Heat oil in a wok until it is smoking — this will only take a few seconds. Add spring onion, garlic and ginger and stir for a few seconds. Next, add chicken and stir it around until it has all turned white. Add the red capsicum and keep stirring, then throw in the snow peas and cashews and stir-fry for another minute or so.

Once the red capsicum has started to soften a little, add the soy sauce and sesame oil, toss everything together and then tip the stir-fry out into a serving dish.

Serve with rice or noodles and more soy sauce if you like.

Serves 1

Minestrone with pesto

1 tablespoon olive oil
1 small onion, finely chopped
1 garlic clove, finely chopped
1 tablespoon finely chopped parsley
55 g (1¾ oz) pancetta, cubed
1 small celery stalk, halved, then sliced
1 small carrot, sliced
1 teaspoon tomato paste (purée)
200 g (7 oz) tinned chopped tomatoes
1 litre (44 fl oz/4 cups) chicken or vegetable stock
1 small zucchini (courgette), sliced
40 g (1½ oz/¼ cup) fresh or frozen peas
4 runner beans, cut into 2 cm (¾ inch) lengths
a handful shredded savoy cabbage
2 tablespoons ditalini pasta
300 g (10½ oz) tinned borlotti beans, drained and rinsed
fresh pesto, to serve

Note: Leftover soup can be frozen.

Heat the oil in a large saucepan and add the onion, garlic, parsley and pancetta. Cook everything over a very low heat, stirring the mixture once or twice, for about 10 minutes, or until the onion is soft and golden. If your heat won't go very low, keep an eye on everything and stir more often.

Add the celery and carrot and cook for 5 minutes. Stir in the tomato paste and chopped tomato with plenty of pepper. Add stock and bring slowly to the boil. Cover and leave to simmer for 30 minutes, stirring once or twice.

Taste the soup for seasoning, adjust if necessary, then add the zucchini, peas, runner beans, cabbage, ditalini and borlotti beans. Simmer about 10 more minutes until the pasta is al dente. For a single serve, spoon some pesto into the middle of a bowl of minestrone.

Makes about 7 cups/portions

Spaghetti puttanesca

100 g (3½ oz) spaghetti
1 tablespoon olive oil
1 small onion, finely chopped
1 garlic clove, finely sliced
¼ small red chilli, cored, seeded and sliced
1–2 anchovy fillets, finely chopped
200 g (7 oz) tinned chopped tomatoes or passata sauce
2 teaspoons finely chopped fresh oregano
about 6 black olives, halved and pitted
1 tablespoon baby capers
a small handful basil leaves

Cook spaghetti in a large saucepan of boiling, salted water until al dente, stirring once or twice to make sure pieces are not stuck together. The cooking time will vary depending on brand of spaghetti. Check the pasta occasionally as it cooks because the time given on packet instructions is often too long by a minute or two.

Heat the olive oil in a saucepan and add the onion, garlic and chilli. Gently fry for about 8 minutes, or until onion is soft. Add anchovies and cook for another minute. Add tomato, oregano, olive halves and capers and bring to the boil. Reduce heat, season with salt and pepper, and leave the sauce to simmer for 3 minutes.

Drain the spaghetti and add it to the sauce. Toss together well so that the pasta is coated in the sauce. Scatter the basil over the top and serve.

Serves 1

Prawn laksa

3 teaspoons oil
1 tablespoon laksa paste
125 ml (4 fl oz/½ cup) coconut milk
125 ml (4 fl oz/½ cup) chicken stock
4–6 prawns (shrimp), peeled and deveined
60 g (1 bundle) rice vermicelli
2 bean curd puffs, cut into 3 pieces
3 cm (1¼ inch) piece cucumber, cut into shreds
1 handful bean sprouts
a few sprigs Vietnamese mint or mint leaves
sambal oelek
lime wedges

Heat the oil in a wok or saucepan and add the laksa paste (depending on the brand, you may need to add a little more or less than the recipe says – you can only find this out by trial and error, so start with a little, make up the soup base and then stir in a bit more if you need to). Cook the paste over a medium heat, stirring it to stop it from sticking, for 2 to 3 minutes.

Stir in the coconut milk and chicken stock, bring mixture to the boil and simmer for 5 minutes. Add prawns, bring the mixture back to the boil, then reduce the heat and simmer for 3 minutes – the prawns will turn pink and opaque when they are ready.

Cook rice vermicelli in boiling water for 3 minutes. Drain and put in a deep serving bowl.

Add bean curd puffs, cucumber and bean sprouts to the bowl, then ladle in the laksa mixture. Garnish the laksa with a sprig or two of Vietnamese mint and a small amount of sambal oelek (be careful as it is very hot). Serve with lime wedges to squeeze into laksa.

Serves 1

Asparagus risotto

250 g (9 oz) asparagus
375 ml (13 fl oz/1½ cups) chicken stock
1 tablespoon olive oil
1 small onion, finely chopped
110 g (3¾ oz/½ cup) arborio rice
2 tablespoons parmesan cheese, grated
2 tablespoons thick (double/heavy) cream

Wash the asparagus and remove the woody ends. Separate the tender tips from the stems.

Cook the asparagus stems in boiling water for about 5 minutes, or until very tender. Drain and put in a blender with the chicken stock. Blend for 1 minute, then put in a saucepan, bring to the boil and maintain at a low simmer.

Cook the asparagus tips in boiling water for 1 minute, drain and refresh in iced water. Set aside.

Heat the olive oil in a heavy-based saucepan. Add the onion and cook until softened but not browned. Add the rice and reduce the heat to low. Season and stir briefly to thoroughly coat the rice. Stir in a ladleful of the simmering stock and then cook over moderate heat, stirring continuously. When the stock has been absorbed, stir in another ladleful. Continue this process for about 20 minutes, until all stock has been added and rice is al dente. Add a little more stock or water if necessary.

Add parmesan cheese and cream, and gently stir in the asparagus tips. Season with salt and pepper, and serve hot.

Serves 1

Baked potato with rocket, broad beans and blue cheese

1 large potato
coarse salt
60 g (2¼ oz/⅓ cup) broad (fava) beans
2 tablespoons cream
30 g (1 oz) blue cheese, crumbled
1 small handful rocket (arugula), chopped

Pre heat oven to 200°C (400°F/Gas 6). Wash the potato and, while it is still damp, rub with a little of the coarse salt. Prick several times and then put in the oven, sitting directly on the oven shelf. This will help get a good all-round heat. Bake for 1 hour, then squeeze gently — it should be soft. If still hard, give it another 15 minutes or so.

Cook broad beans in boiling water for 3 minutes, then drain them well. Peel off the outer grey skins.

When potato is cooked, cut a cross on top and squeeze potato around the middle until it opens up.

Put cream in a small saucepan, add broad beans, cook them gently for a minute or two, then add the blue cheese and rocket. Stir everything together and when the rocket has wilted, spoon the mixture into the potato. Season with black pepper.

Serves 1

Salmon kedgeree

330 ml (11¼ fl oz/1⅓ cups) fish stock
125 g (4½ oz) boneless salmon fillet
1½ tablespoons butter
2 teaspoons oil
1 small onion, chopped
1 teaspoon madras curry paste
65 g (2¼ oz/⅓ cup) long-grain rice
1 tablespoon chopped parsley
1 tablespoon cream
1 hard-boiled egg, cut into wedges
lemon wedges, to serve

Put the stock in a small saucepan and bring to the boil. Put the salmon in the stock, cover, then reduce the heat to a simmer. Cook for 3 minutes, or until it becomes firm when pressed and turns opaque. Lift out the salmon and flake it into large pieces by gently pulling it apart with your hands.

Melt 1 tablespoon of butter and oil in a small frying pan (skillet), add onion and cook over a low heat until onion softens and turns translucent. Stir in curry paste, then add rice and mix well until rice is coated. Add fish stock, mix well, then bring the mixture to the boil.

Simmer the rice, covered, over a very low heat for 8 minutes, then add salmon and cook, covered, for another 5 minutes, until all liquid is absorbed. If the rice is too dry and not cooked, add a splash of boiling water and keep cooking for a further 1–2 minutes.

Stir in rest of the butter, parsley and cream (you can leave out the cream if you prefer — the results won't be so rich). Serve kedgeree with the egg wedges on top and lemon wedges to squeeze over.

Serves 1

Spicy sausages with harissa and couscous

2 teaspoons butter
95 g (3¼ oz/½ cup) instant couscous
¼–½ teaspoon harissa, to taste
1½ tablespoons olive oil
1 tablespoon lemon juice
2 teaspoons grated lemon zest
1 tablespoon chopped parsley
50 g (1¾ oz) chargrilled red capsicum (pepper), sliced
1 tablespoon raisins
2–3 merguez sausages
thick plain yoghurt, to serve

Put the butter in a small saucepan with 170 ml (5½ fl oz/⅔ cup) water and bring to the boil. Sprinkle in the couscous, mix it into the water, then take it off the stove. Put a lid on the pan and leave it to sit for 5 minutes. Turn on the grill (broiler).

In a bowl, stir the harissa, the olive oil, lemon juice and zest together until well mixed. Add parsley, red capsicum and raisins and leave everything to marinate briefly.

Grill sausages for 8 minutes, turning them so they brown on all sides.

Meanwhile, take lid off the couscous, stir it for a minute or two to separate the grains, then stir in harissa mixture.

Serve the couscous with the sausages sliced over it and topped with a large dollop of yoghurt.

Serves 1

Tomato risotto

375 ml (13 fl oz/1½ cups) chicken or vegetable stock
a pinch saffron threads
80 ml (2½ fl oz/⅓ cup) dry white wine
1 tablespoon butter
1 small onion, finely chopped
110 g (3¾ oz/½ cup) arborio rice
2 teaspoons olive oil
1 small garlic clove, crushed
125 g (4½ oz) (about 15) cherry tomatoes
parmesan cheese, grated
1 tablespoon finely chopped parsley

Heat stock in a small saucepan until it is simmering, then leave it over a low heat. Put the saffron into the wine and leave it to soak.

Melt butter in a heavy-based saucepan, then gently cook onion until soft, but not browned. Add rice, turn the heat to low and stir well to coat all the grains of rice in the butter.

Add wine and saffron to the rice, turn heat up to medium and cook, stirring rice, until all liquid has been absorbed. Add hot stock, a couple of ladles at a time, stirring continuously so that the rice cooks evenly and releases some of its starch.

While the rice is cooking, heat oil in a small frying pan (skillet), add garlic and tomatoes, then fry for 2 to 3 minutes over medium heat until the tomatoes are slightly soft and have burst open. Season well.

Once all stock has been added to the rice, taste the rice to see if it is al dente, adding a little more stock or water if necessary. Stir in 2 tablespoons of the parmesan and the parsley. Spoon the tomatoes over the top and scatter more parmesan on top. Serve straight away.

Serves 1

Hamburger with fresh corn relish

150 g (5 oz) minced (ground) beef
1 garlic clove, crushed
1 small onion, very finely chopped
1 tablespoon finely chopped parsley
2 teaspoons tomato ketchup
2 drops worcestershire sauce
1 corn cob
1 tomato, finely chopped
2 teaspoons sweet chilli sauce
1 tablespoon chopped coriander (cilantro) leaves
2 teaspoons lime juice
2 teaspoons olive oil
1 hamburger bun
few baby cos (romaine) leaves

Turn on the grill (broiler). Put beef in a bowl with the garlic, half of the onion, the parsley, tomato ketchup and the worcestershire sauce. Season and mix well, then leave it to marinate while you make the relish.

Grill the corn cob on all sides until it is slightly blackened and charred around the edges. By this time it should be cooked through. Slice off kernels by slicing down the length of the cob with a sharp knife. Mix kernels with tomato, chilli sauce, coriander and remaining onion. Add lime juice, salt and pepper to taste.

Form the beef mixture into a large patty and flatten out to the size of the bun (bear in mind that it will shrink as it cooks).

Heat oil in a non-stick frying pan (skillet) and fry beef patty for 3–5 minutes on each side, depending on how well cooked you like it. While it is cooking, toast the bun.

Lay a lettuce leaf or two on the bun bottom, add some of the corn relish and top with the hamburger patty and the bun top. Serve any extra relish on the side.

Serves 1

Roast baby potatoes with sweet chilli dip

200 g (7 oz) baby potatoes
1 tablespoon olive oil
1 teaspoon thyme leaves
1 teaspoon coarse salt
2 tablespoons sweet chilli sauce
2 tablespoons sour cream
1 spring onion (scallion), finely chopped

Put oven on to 200°C (400°F/Gas 6). If any of your potatoes are too big to eat in more than two bites, cut them in half. Put them in a roasting tin with the oil, thyme and salt and mix them around so they are all coated. Roast for 30 to 40 minutes, tossing once or twice, or until potatoes are cooked all the way through.

In a small bowl, mix the sweet chilli sauce, sour cream and spring onion together. Serve with the potatoes as a dipping sauce.

Serves 1

Tandoori chicken with cardamom rice

80 ml (2½ fl oz/⅓ cup) natural yoghurt, plus extra for serving
1 tablespoon tandoori paste
3 teaspoons lemon juice
2 small boneless, skinless chicken breasts, cut into 4 cm (1½ inch) cubes
2 teaspoons oil
½ small onion, finely diced
100 g (3½ oz/½ cup) long-grain rice
1 cardamom pod, bruised
250 ml (9 fl oz/1 cup) hot chicken stock
125 g (4½ oz) English spinach leaves

Soak two wooden skewers in water for about 30 minutes to prevent them burning during cooking (or use metal skewers). Combine yoghurt, tandoori paste and the lemon juice in a non-metallic dish. Add chicken and coat well, then cover and marinate for at least 10 minutes.

Meanwhile, heat the oil in a small saucepan. Add the onion and cook for 3 minutes, then add the rice and cardamom pod. Cook, stirring often, for 2–3 minutes, or until the rice is slightly opaque. Add the hot chicken stock and bring to the boil. Reduce the heat to low, cover, and cook the rice, without removing the lid, for 15 minutes.

Heat a barbecue plate or oven grill (broiler) to very hot. Thread chicken cubes onto skewers. Cook on each side for about 5 minutes, or until cooked through.

Wash spinach and put in a saucepan with just the water clinging to the leaves. Cook, covered, over medium heat for 1–2 minutes, or until spinach has wilted. Uncover the rice, fluff up with a fork and serve with the spinach, chicken and extra yoghurt.

Serves 1

Ham braised with witlof

3 teaspoons oil
1 teaspoon butter
1 witlof (chicory/Belgian endive) head, sliced horizontally
2 thick slices leg ham
1 teaspoon brown sugar
60 ml (2 fl oz/¼ cup) white wine
1 tablespoon finely chopped parsley

Heat oil in a frying pan (skillet), add the butter and when it is sizzling, add the witlof, with the cut-side down, and fry for a minute. Add the slices of ham to the pan and fry them briefly on each side, moving witlof to one side. Add the sugar and wine to the pan, season well and cover it with a lid. Cook for 3 minutes, or until the witlof is soft.

Take the lid off the pan, turn the heat up and let the sauce bubble until it has thickened and gone quite sticky. Scatter over the parsley.

Serves 1

Cauliflower rarebit

2 thick slices ciabatta
1 garlic clove
150 g (5½ oz) cauliflower, cut into small florets
2 tablespoons grated gruyère cheese
2 tablespoons grated cheddar cheese
1 teaspoon dijon mustard
1 egg, beaten
1 tablespoon beer
2 tablespoons pouring cream

Turn on the grill (broiler) and toast the ciabatta. Cut the garlic clove in half and rub the cut sides over one side of each slice of ciabatta.

Bring a saucepan of water to the boil and cook cauliflower florets for about 5 minutes, or until tender when you prod it them with a knife. Drain well.

Mix the cheeses, mustard, egg, beer and cream together. Put the toast on a baking tray and arrange some of the cauliflower on top of each piece. Divide the cheese mixture over the pieces of toast, making sure you coat all the cauliflower.

Put the rarebits under the grill and grill them until brown and bubbling.

Serves 1

Chicken casserole with olives and tomatoes

3 teaspoons olive oil
1 small onion, chopped
1 garlic clove, crushed
2–3 pieces chicken (such as thigh fillets or drumsticks), skin on
2 teaspoons tomato paste (purée)
125 ml (4 fl oz/½ cup) white wine
a pinch of sugar
2 large ripe tomatoes, peeled and chopped
1 tablespoon chopped parsley
50 g (1¾ oz) green beans, topped, tailed and halved
45 g (1½ oz/¼ cup) olives

Heat the oil in a small flameproof casserole and fry onion for a minute or two. Add the garlic and the chicken and fry for as long as it takes to brown the chicken all over.

Add tomato paste and white wine, along with sugar, and stir everything together. Add tomato and any juices, the parsley and beans and bring to the boil. Turn down heat, season well and simmer for 30 minutes.

Add the olives and simmer for another 5 minutes. The sauce should be thick by now and the chicken fully cooked. Add more salt and pepper, if desired. Serve with potatoes, pasta or rice.

Serves 1

Salsicce with white beans and gremolata

1 tablespoon olive oil
2 salsicce or thick pork sausages, cut into chunks
3 garlic cloves
85 g (3 oz) chargrilled red or yellow capsicum (pepper)
300 g (10½ oz) tinned cannellini beans, drained and rinsed
2 teaspoons grated lemon zest
2 tablespoons chopped parsley
2 teaspoons lemon juice
extra virgin olive oil, for drizzling

Heat olive oil in a frying pan (skillet) and cook the salsicce until they are browned all over and cooked through. Lift them out of the frying pan (skillet) with a slotted spoon and put them to one side.

Thinly slice two of the garlic cloves, add them to the frying pan and cook over a gentle heat until very soft. Cut capsicum into strips and add to the pan, along with beans and salsicce. Stir together and cook over a gentle heat for 2 minutes to heat salsicce through. Season well with salt and freshly ground black pepper.

To make the gremolata, smash the remaining garlic clove to a paste, with a little salt, in a mortar and pestle. Mix in lemon zest and chopped parsley and season with salt and pepper.

Just before serving, stir the gremolata through the beans, pile onto a serving plate and then finish the dish with the lemon juice and a drizzle of olive oil.

Serves 1

Stir-fried tofu with oyster sauce

150 g (5 oz) firm tofu
1 tablespoon oil
1 garlic clove, crushed
1 teaspoon grated ginger
1 tablespoon oyster sauce
1 tablespoon soy sauce
1 teaspoon sugar
2 oyster mushroom, quartered
1 spring onion (scallion), cut into pieces
1 baby bok choy (pak choi), trimmed and quartered
a small handful coriander (cilantro) leaves

Cut the tofu into bite-sized pieces. Pat dry with paper towels. Heat a wok over a medium heat, add the oil and heat until it is very hot and almost smoking. Cook the tofu until golden brown on all sides, making sure you move it around gently or it will stick and break.

Add the garlic, the ginger, the oyster sauce, the soy sauce and the sugar, then toss until well combined. Add the oyster mushrooms, spring onion and bok choy, then simmer until the sauce has reduced a little and spring onion and bok choy have softened slightly. Garnish with coriander leaves.

Serves 1

Chive gnocchi with blue cheese

225 g (8 oz) floury potatoes
about 75 g (2½ oz/½ cup) plain (all-purpose) flour
1 tablespoon chopped chives
1 egg yolk
30 g (1 oz) blue cheese
2 tablespoons thick cream

Peel the potatoes and cut them into even-sized pieces. Cook in simmering water for 15 minutes, or until tender. Drain them very well, then mash in a large bowl. Add most of the flour, the chives and egg yolk, along with some seasoning, and mix well. Now add enough remaining flour to make a mixture that is soft but not sticky. Roll into a sausage shape 2.5 cm (1 inch) across and cut off lengths about 1.5 cm (⅝ inch) long. You don't need to shape gnocchi any more than this.

Bring a saucepan of water to the boil and cook gnocchi. As it rises to the surface (it will do this when it is cooked through), scoop it out with a slotted spoon and drain well.

While the gnocchi are cooking, put the blue cheese and cream in a small saucepan and gently heat together. Put gnocchi in a large serving bowl and pour blue cheese sauce over it. Gently fold sauce into the gnocchi and serve.

Serves 1

Pastitsio

1 tablespoon oil
1 garlic clove, crushed
1 small onion, chopped
250 g (9 oz) minced (ground) beef
250 g (9 oz) tinned chopped tomatoes
60 ml (2 fl oz/¼ cup) dry red wine
60 ml (2 fl oz/¼ cup) beef stock
1 bay leaf
½ teaspoon dried mixed herbs
85 g (3 oz) ziti pasta
2 eggs, lightly beaten
125 g (4½ oz/½ cup) Greek-style yoghurt
50 g (1¾ oz) kefalotyri cheese, grated
pinch ground nutmeg
2 tablespoons grated cheddar cheese
lettuce salad, to serve

Note: Cover the remaining pastitsio with foil and refrigerate for up to 2 days. Reheat as needed.

Heat oil in a heavy-based pan, and cook garlic and onion over medium heat for 5 minutes, or until the onion is soft. Add the beef and cook over high heat until browned, mashing to break up any lumps. Add the tomato, wine, stock, bay leaf and herbs and bring to the boil. Reduce the heat and simmer for 40 minutes. Season well.

Preheat the oven to 180°C (350°F/Gas 4). Meanwhile, cook the pasta in a saucepan of rapidly boiling water until al dente. Drain well and spread in the base of a 1 litre (35 fl oz/4 cups) ovenproof dish. Pour in half the egg and top with the meat sauce.

Combine the yoghurt, remaining egg, kefalotyri and nutmeg and pour over the top. Sprinkle with cheddar. Bake for 30 minutes, or until golden brown. Leave to stand for 10 minutes before serving a portion with lettuce salad.

Makes 2–3 serves/portions

Spinach and ricotta ravioli

3 teaspoons olive oil
½ small red onion, finely chopped
1 garlic clove, crushed
50 g (about a large handful) baby English spinach leaves, coarsely chopped
60 g (2¼ oz/¼ cup) ricotta cheese
1 egg yolk
1 tablespoon grated parmesan cheese
freshly grated nutmeg
about 12 won ton wrappers
1 tablespoon butter
6–8 sage leaves

Heat oil in a small frying pan (skillet), add the onion and garlic and fry them over a low heat for a few minutes until onion goes soft and translucent. Add spinach and stir it around until it wilts.

Stir spinach mixture into the ricotta, along with the egg yolk, parmesan, some nutmeg and salt and pepper.

Brush a little water around edge of a won ton wrapper and put a teaspoon of filling in the centre. Fold wrapper over to make a half moon shape and press the edges firmly together. Put the ravioli on a tea towel laid out on your work surface and repeat with the remaining wrappers.

Bring a saucepan of water to the boil and cook the ravioli for a few minutes. They will float to the surface when ready. Scoop them out carefully with a slotted spoon and drain in a colander. Melt butter in a small saucepan, add sage and sizzle for a few minutes until butter browns slightly. Put ravioli into a bowl and pour the butter and sage over them. Serve at once.

Serves 1

Egg fried rice

1 egg
1 spring onion (scallion), chopped
40 g (1½ oz/¼ cup) fresh or frozen peas
1 tablespoon oil
280 g (10 oz/1½ cups) cooked long-grain rice
oyster sauce or ketjap manis, to drizzle

Note: 100 g (3½ oz/½ cup) uncooked long-grain rice will produce about 280 g (10 oz/1½ cups) cooked rice.

Beat the egg with a pinch of salt and 1 teaspoon of the spring onion. Cook peas in a pan of simmering water for 3 minutes if fresh or 1 minute if frozen.

Heat a wok over high heat, add the oil and heat until very hot. Reduce heat, add the egg and lightly scramble. Add rice before the egg is completely set. Increase the heat, then stir to separate the rice grains and break the egg into small bits.

Add peas and remaining spring onion. Season with salt. Stir constantly for 1 minute. Serve drizzled with sauce.

Serves 1

Grilled nachos

150 g (5½ oz) packet corn chips
1 tomato, chopped
¼ small red onion, finely chopped
½ jalapeño chilli, thinly sliced
2 teaspoons lime juice
1 tablespoon chopped coriander (cilantro) leaves
50 g (1¾ oz/⅓ cup) crumbled feta cheese

Turn on the grill (broiler). Arrange the corn chips on an ovenproof plate.

Scatter the tomato, onion and chilli on top of the corn chips, then drizzle with the lime juice and season with some salt. Scatter coriander and feta cheese over the top, making sure corn chips are well covered.

Grill nachos until they start to brown around edges and the cheese starts to melt. Serve hot but be careful of the plate — it will be very hot, too.

Serves 1

Ramen noodle soup with char siu

75 g (2 nests) dried thin ramen egg noodles
375 ml (13 fl oz/1½ cups) chicken stock
1 spring onion (scallion), shredded
1 tablespoon soy sauce
100 g (3½ oz) piece of char siu
1 baby bok choy (pak choy), trimmed and roughly chopped
sesame oil, for drizzling

Note: Instead of the char siu, you can add a cooked and sliced chicken fillet or a portion of barbecued duck.

Cook noodles in a medium saucepan of boiling salted water for 4 minutes, or until they are just cooked, stirring once or twice to make sure they are not stuck together. Cooking time will vary depending on brand of noodles.

Bring the chicken stock to the boil in a small saucepan, then add the spring onion and soy sauce. Taste stock to see if it has enough flavour and, if not, add a bit more soy sauce — don't overdo it though as the soup's base should be quite mild in flavour. Turn heat down to a simmer. Cut the char siu into bite-sized shreds or slices (small enough to eat with chopsticks).

Drain noodles and place in a deep serving bowl. Add bok choy to the chicken stock, stir it in, then add the stock and the vegetables to the bowl. Arrange char siu on top, then drizzle a little sesame oil over — sesame oil has a very strong flavour, so only a couple of drops are needed.

Serves 1

Hot and sweet chicken

1½ tablespoons rice vinegar
2 tablespoons caster (superfine) sugar
2 small garlic cloves, crushed
a small pinch of chilli flakes
½ teaspoon ground coriander
½ teaspoon ground white pepper
a handful of coriander (cilantro), finely chopped, including roots and stems
1½ tablespoons olive oil
1 tablespoon lemon juice
2 boneless and skinless chicken thighs, cut in half
2 teaspoons caster (superfine) sugar, extra
2 teaspoons fish sauce
½ small cucumber, peeled and sliced

Put the vinegar and sugar in a small saucepan, bring to the boil, then turn down the heat and simmer for a minute. Take the mixture off the heat and add half of the crushed garlic cloves, the chilli flakes and a pinch of salt. Leave the dressing to cool.

Heat a small frying pan (skillet) for a minute, add the ground coriander and white pepper and stir it around for a minute. This will make the spices more fragrant. Add remaining garlic, fresh coriander and a pinch of salt. Add 1 tablespoon of oil and all the lemon juice and mix to a paste. Rub this all over the chicken pieces.

Heat rest of the oil in a wok, add the chicken and fry it on both sides for 8 minutes, or until cooked through. Sprinkle in extra sugar and the fish sauce and cook for another minute or two until any excess liquid has evaporated and chicken pieces are sticky. Serve the chicken with the sliced cucumber and some rice. Dress with the sauce.

Serves 1

Lamb pilaff

125 g (4½ oz) eggplant (aubergine), cut into 1 cm (½ inch) cubes
2½ tablespoons olive oil
1 small onion, finely chopped
1 teaspoon ground cumin
½ teaspoon ground cinnamon
½ teaspoon ground coriander
100 g (3½ oz/½ cup) long-grain rice
250 ml (7 fl oz/1 cup) chicken or vegetable stock
150 g (5½ oz) minced (ground) lamb
¼ teaspoon allspice
2 teaspoons olive oil, extra, for frying
1 tomato, cut into wedges
1 tablespoon toasted pistachios
1 tablespoon currants
1 tablespoon chopped coriander (cilantro) leaves, to garnish

Put eggplant in a colander, sprinkle with salt and leave for 1 hour. Rinse and squeeze dry. Heat 2 tablespoons of oil in a small frying pan (skillet), add the eggplant and then cook over medium heat for 5–6 minutes. Drain on paper towels.

In a small saucepan, heat remaining oil, add the onion and then cook for 4–5 minutes, or until soft. Stir in half each of the cumin, the cinnamon and ground coriander. Add rice and stir to coat, then add the stock, season and bring to the boil. Reduce the heat and simmer, covered, for 15 minutes.

Put lamb in a bowl with the allspice and remaining cumin, cinnamon and ground coriander. Season with salt and pepper, and mix. Roll into balls the size of macadamia nuts. Heat 2 teaspoons of oil in the frying pan and cook the meatballs over medium heat for 5 minutes. Drain on paper towels.

Add the tomato to the pan and cook, for 2–3 minutes, or until it is golden. Remove from the pan. Stir eggplant, pistachios, currants and meatballs through the rice. Serve pilaff with the tomato and coriander.

Serves 1

Saffron chicken and rice

1 tablespoon olive oil
1–2 chicken thighs and 2 drumsticks
1 small red onion, finely chopped
1 small green capsicum (pepper), two-thirds diced and one-third cut into very thin slices
1 teaspoon sweet paprika
200 g (7 oz) tinned chopped tomatoes
135 g (4¾ oz/⅔ cup) long-grain rice
¼ teaspoon ground saffron

Note: Leftover rice and chicken will keep, covered and refrigerated, for 2 days. Reheat in a microwave. This dish is good reheated the next day.

Heat half of the oil in a deep frying pan (skillet) over high heat. Pat the chicken pieces dry with paper towels. Season chicken pieces well. Cook until evenly browned all over. Remove the chicken from the pan.

Reduce the heat to medium and add the remaining oil. Add the onion and diced capsicum, and cook gently for 5 minutes. Stir in paprika and cook for about 30 seconds. Add tomato and simmer for 1–3 minutes, or until the mixture thickens.

Stir 435 ml (15¼ fl oz/1¾ cups) boiling water into the pan, add rice and saffron. Return chicken to pan and stir to combine. Season with salt and pepper. Bring to the boil, cover, reduce the heat to medium–low and simmer for 20 minutes, or until all the liquid has been absorbed and chicken is tender. Stir in thinly sliced capsicum; leave to stand, covered, for 3–4 minutes. For 1 serve, spoon a portion into a serving bowl.

Makes 2 serves/portions

Porcini and walnut pasta

5 g (⅛ oz) porcini
100 g (3½ oz) penne
1 tablespoon olive oil
1 small onion, finely chopped
1 garlic clove, crushed
8 button mushrooms, sliced
1 thyme sprig
35 g (1¼ oz/⅓ cup) walnuts
1 tablespoon sour cream
parmesan cheese, grated

Put porcini in a bowl with just enough boiling water to cover them and leave to soak for half an hour. If they soak up all the water very quickly, add a little more.

Cook penne in a large saucepan of boiling salted water until it is al dente, stirring once or twice to make sure the pieces are not stuck together. The cooking time will vary, depending on brand of pasta. Check the pasta occasionally as it cooks because the packet instructions are often too long by a minute or two. Drain and then return the pasta to the saucepan.

Heat the oil in a frying pan (skillet) and fry the onion and garlic together until translucent but not browned. Add the porcini, any soaking liquid, mushrooms and thyme, and keep frying. The mushrooms will give off liquid as they cook so keep cooking until they soak it up again.

In a small separate frying pan (skillet), fry walnuts without any oil until they start to brown and smell toasted. When they have cooled a bit, roughly chop them and add to mushrooms. Toss sauce through penne, stir the sour cream through and season well. Serve with the parmesan.

Serves 1

Thai basil fried rice

1 tablespoon oil
2 Asian shallots, sliced
1 garlic clove, finely chopped
½ small red chilli, seeded and finely chopped
50 g (1¾ oz) snake or green beans, cut into short pieces
½ small red capsicum (pepper), cut into batons
50 g (1¾ oz) button mushrooms, halved
280 g (10 oz/1½ cups) cooked jasmine rice
½ teaspoon grated palm sugar
1½ tablespoons light soy sauce
1 tablespoon Thai basil, shredded
1 tablespoon coriander (cilantro) leaves, chopped
fried red Asian shallot flakes, to garnish
Thai basil leaves, to garnish

Note: 100 g (3½ oz/½ cup) uncooked rice will give you about 280 (10 oz/1½ cups) when cooked.

Heat a wok over high heat, add the oil and swirl. Stir-fry the shallots, garlic and chilli for 3 minutes, or until the shallots start to brown. Add the beans, capsicum and mushrooms, stir-fry for 3 minutes, or until cooked, then stir in the cooked jasmine rice and heat through.

Dissolve the palm sugar in the soy sauce, then pour over the rice. Stir in the herbs. Garnish with the shallot flakes and basil.

Serves 1

Roast vegetables with poached egg and camembert

3 baby onions or French shallots
2 tablespoons olive oil
1 bundle asparagus, trimmed and cut into 4 cm (1½ inch) pieces
1 zucchini (courgette), thickly sliced
1 baby eggplant (aubergine), sliced
2 garlic cloves
1 tablespoon lemon juice
1 egg
55 g (2 oz) camembert cheese, cubed

Preheat the oven to 200°C (400°F/ Gas 6). Peel the baby onions, leaving them still attached at the root end. Don't leave any root on.

Put oil in a roasting tin and add the onions, asparagus, zucchini, eggplant, and garlic, and toss well. Season with salt and black pepper. Put the tin in the oven and roast the vegetables for 20 minutes. Remove the garlic cloves. Sprinkle on the lemon juice and roast for another 10 minutes.

Put a small saucepan full of water over a high heat and bring it to the boil. When the water is bubbling, turn heat down to a gentle simmer. Crack egg into a cup and slip it into the water — it should start to turn opaque. Turn heat down as low as you can and leave for 3 minutes.

Pile the vegetables into an ovenproof serving dish. Squeeze roasted garlic over vegetables. Put the camembert on top of vegetables. Put dish back in the oven for a couple of minutes to start the cheese melting.

Top with the poached egg and some black pepper.

Serves 1

Chilli linguine with chermoula chicken

2 teaspoons olive oil
1 boneless, skinless chicken breast
100 g (3½ oz) chilli linguine

Chermoula
1 large handful coriander (cilantro), leaves, chopped
1 large handful flat-leaf (Italian) parsley leaves, chopped
1 garlic clove, crushed
1 teaspoon ground cumin
1 teaspoon ground paprika
60 ml (2 fl oz/¼ cup) lemon juice
1 teaspoon lemon zest
60 ml (2 fl oz/¼ cup) olive oil

Heat the oil in a small non-stick frying pan (skillet) over medium heat. Add chicken breast and cook until tender. Remove from pan and then leave for about 5 minutes before cutting into thin slices.

Cook the pasta in a large saucepan of rapidly boiling salted water until al dente, then drain.

Meanwhile, combine the chermoula ingredients in a glass bowl and add the sliced chicken. Leave to stand until the pasta has finished cooking. Serve the pasta topped with the chermoula and chicken.

Serves 1

Green chicken curry

80 ml (2½ fl oz/⅓ cup) coconut cream
1 tablespoon green curry paste
2 skinless chicken thighs or 1 skinless chicken breast, cut into pieces
80 ml (2½ fl oz/⅓ cup) coconut milk
1 Thai eggplant or a baby purple eggplant (aubergine), cut into chunks
3 teaspoons shaved palm sugar or brown sugar
3 teaspoons fish sauce
1 makrut (kaffir lime) leaf, torn
a small handful Thai basil leaves
½ small red chilli, sliced
coconut milk or cream, for drizzling

Put a wok over a low heat, add the coconut cream and let it come to the boil. Stir it for a while until the oil separates out. Don't let it burn.

Add the green curry paste, stir for a minute, then add the chicken. Cook the chicken until it turns opaque, then add the coconut milk and eggplant. Cook for several more minutes until the eggplant is tender. Add the sugar, fish sauce, lime leaves and half of the basil, then mix together.

Garnish with the rest of the basil, the chilli and a drizzle of coconut milk or cream. Serve with rice.

Serves 1

Beef ball and white bean soup

150 g (5½ oz) minced (ground) beef
1 garlic clove, crushed
1 tablespoon finely chopped parsley
a pinch ground cinnamon
a pinch freshly grated nutmeg
1 egg, lightly beaten
500 ml (17 fl oz/2 cups) beef stock
1 small carrot, thinly sliced
300 g (10½ oz) tinned white beans, drained
75 g (2½ oz/1 cup) finely shredded savoy cabbage
Parmesan cheese, grated

Note: Cover and refrigerate leftover soup. Reheat the next day.

Put the beef in a bowl with garlic, parsley, cinnamon, nutmeg and half of the egg. Mix everything together well and season with salt and pepper. If mixture is dry, add the rest of the egg — you want it to be sticky enough so that forming small balls is easy.

Roll the beef mixture into small balls — they should be small enough to scoop up on a spoon and eat in one mouthful. Put them on a plate as you make them.

Put the beef stock in a saucepan, with the carrot, and bring it to the boil. Add the meatballs, one at a time, and turn the heat down to a simmer. Test one of the balls after 3 minutes. It should be cooked through, so if it isn't, cook for a little longer. Now add beans and cabbage and cook for 4 to 5 minutes. Season the broth to taste.

For a single serve, ladle a portion of the soup and meatballs into a deep bowl and stir in lots of parmesan. Serve with plenty of bread to dunk into the broth.

Makes 2 serves/portions

Sweet and sour pork

150 g (5½ oz) pork loin, cubed
1 egg, lightly beaten
1½ tablespoons cornflour (cornstarch)
1 tablespoon oil
1 small onion, cubed
½ red capsicum (pepper), cubed
1 spring onion (scallion), cut into lengths
60 ml (2 fl oz/¼ cup) clear rice vinegar or white vinegar
1 tablespoon tomato ketchup
55 g (2 oz/¼ cup) sugar
1 tablespoon oil, extra

Note: Cover and refrigerate any leftover Sweet and Sour Pork. Gently reheat the next day.

Put the pork cubes and egg in a bowl with 1 tablespoon of the cornflour. Stir everything around to coat the pork well.

Heat a wok over a high heat, add half of the oil and heat it until it just starts to smoke. Add onion and cook it for a minute. Add red capsicum and spring onion and cook for another minute. Add rice vinegar, tomato ketchup and sugar, turn down heat and stir together until sugar dissolves. Bring to the boil and simmer for about 3 minutes.

Mix the remaining cornflour with 1 tablespoon of water, add it to sweet-and-sour mixture, then simmer for a minute until sauce thickens a bit. Pour the sauce into a bowl.

Heat extra oil in a non-stick frying pan (skillet) over a medium heat. As soon as oil is hot, slide pork cubes into pan and cook until browned and crisp. Remove from pan. Add the sauce and reheat everything until the sauce is bubbling. Spoon a serving portion into a deep bowl. Serve with the rice or noodles.

Serves 1

Nasi goreng

1 small egg
1½ tablespoons oil
1 garlic clove, finely chopped
½ small onion, finely chopped
½ small red chilli, seeded and very finely chopped
½ teaspoon shrimp paste
½ teaspoon coriander seeds
pinch sugar
100 g (3½ oz) raw prawns (shrimp), peeled and deveined
50 g (1¾ oz) rump steak, finely sliced
280 g (10 oz/1½ cups) cooked and cooled long-grain rice
1 teaspoon kecap manis
2 teaspoons soy sauce
1 spring onion (scallion), finely chopped
1 cup finely shredded lettuce
¼ small cucumber, thinly sliced
1 tablespoon crisp fried onions

Note: 100 g (3½ oz/½ cup) uncooked long grain rice will give you about 280 g1(0 oz/1½ cups) when cooked.

Beat egg and a pinch of salt until foamy. Heat a frying pan (skillet) or wok and brush with a little oil. Pour the egg into pan in a thin layer and cook for 1–2 minutes over medium heat, or until omelette sets. Turn over and cook the other side for about 30 seconds. Remove from the pan. When omelette is cold, roll up, cut into fine strips and set aside.

Combine garlic, onion, chilli, shrimp paste, coriander and sugar in a mortar and pestle or small food processor, and process until a paste is formed.

Heat 1 tablespoon of the oil in a wok; add paste and cook over high heat for 1 minute. Add the prawns and steak, and stir-fry for 2–3 minutes.

Add remaining oil and cold rice to wok. Stir-fry until the rice is heated through. Add the kecap manis, soy sauce and spring onion, and stir-fry for another minute.

Arrange lettuce around the outside of a serving plate. Put the rice in the centre, and garnish with the omelette, cucumber slices and crisp fried onion. Serve immediately.

Serves 1

Linguine with cherry tomatoes

100 g (3½ oz) linguine
125 g (4½ oz) red cherry tomatoes
125 g (4½ oz) yellow cherry tomatoes
1 tablespoon olive oil
1 garlic clove, crushed
1 spring onion (scallion), sliced
2 tablespoons finely chopped chives
about 6 black olives
extra virgin olive oil, for drizzling

Cook the linguine in a saucepan of boiling salted water until al dente, stirring once or twice to make sure pieces are not stuck together. The cooking time will vary depending on the brand of linguine. Check pasta occasionally as it cooks because the time given on packet instructions is often too long by a minute or two.

Cut cherry tomatoes in half. Heat oil in a saucepan, add garlic and spring onion and let sizzle briefly. Tip in the cherry tomatoes and cook them over a high heat until they just start to collapse and give off their juices. Add chives and olives, season with salt and pepper and toss everything together well.

Drain the linguine and put it in a deep serving bowl. Pour the cherry tomato mixture on top and grind some black pepper over the top. Drizzle with a little bit more olive oil if you like.

Serves 1

Chilli

55 g (2 oz) dried black beans or kidney beans
1 tablespoon oil
1 small red onion, finely chopped
1 garlic clove, crushed
2 handfuls coriander (cilantro), finely chopped
1 small chilli, seeded and finely chopped
400 g (14 oz) chuck steak, cut into small cubes
200 g (7 oz) tinned chopped tomatoes
2 teaspoons tomato paste (purée)
125 ml (4 fl oz/½ cup) beef stock
½ small red capsicum (pepper), cut into squares
1 small ripe tomato, chopped
½ avocado, diced
1 lime, juiced
a dollop of sour cream

Note: Cover and refrigerate remaining chilli. Reheat the next day. Can also be frozen for up to 1 month.

Put dried beans in a saucepan, cover with water, bring to the boil. Reduce heat and simmer 10 minutes. Turn off the heat and leave for 2 hours. Drain and rinse the beans.

In a heatproof casserole dish, heat half the oil. Cook three-quarters of the onion, all the garlic, half the coriander, and the chilli, for 5 minutes.

Remove the onion mixture from the casserole dish and set aside. Heat the remaining oil in the dish, add the steak and cook until well browned. Return the onion to the pan. Add the beans, tinned tomato, tomato paste and stock and stir together. Bring to the boil, then reduce to a simmer. Cook, covered, for 1 hour 20 minutes, adding a little extra stock or water, if needed. Add capsicum and cook for 40 minutes.

For topping, mix half the remaining coriander, the tomato, avocado and remainder of the onion and season well. Add half the lime juice.

When meat is tender, add remaining coriander and lime juice and season well. For 1 serve, spoon a portion into a bowl. Add topping and sour cream.

Makes 2 serves/portions

Lamb curry

400 g (14 oz) lamb leg or shoulder, cubed
60 ml (2 fl oz/¼ cup) thick plain yoghurt
1 small onion, chopped
1 small green chilli, seeded and roughly chopped
1 garlic clove, crushed
2 cm (¾ inch) piece fresh ginger, grated
1 tablespoon cashew nuts
2 tablespoons korma curry paste
1 tablespoon oil

Put the lamb in a bowl with half the yoghurt. Mix until the meat is coated.

Put onion with chilli, garlic, ginger, cashew nuts and curry paste in a blender, add 2 tablespoons of water and process to a smooth paste. If you don't have a blender, finely chop everything before adding the water.

Heat the oil in a heavy-based casserole dish over a medium heat. Add blended mixture, season with salt and cook over a low heat for 1 minute, or until the liquid evaporates and the sauce thickens. Add lamb and slowly bring everything to the boil.

Cover the casserole tightly, simmer for 1 hour and 15 minutes, then add the rest of the yoghurt and cook for another 30 minutes, or until meat is very tender. Stir meat occasionally to prevent it from sticking to pan. The sauce should be quite thick. Serve 1 portion with rice.

Makes 2 serves/portions

Note: Cover and refrigerate remaining curry. Reheat and eat within 3 days. The flavour improves on keeping. This dish can be frozen in an airtight container for up to 1 month.

Grilled chicken with capsicum couscous

60 g (2¼ oz/⅓ cup) instant couscous
2 teaspoons olive oil
1 small onion, finely chopped
1 small zucchini (courgette), sliced
½ small red or yellow chargrilled capsicum (pepper), chopped
3 semi-dried (sun-blushed) tomatoes, chopped
1 teaspoon grated orange zest
80 ml (2½ fl oz/⅓ cup) orange juice
2 tablespoons chopped mint
2 chicken thighs or 1 chicken breast, skin on
2 teaspoons butter, softened

Heat the grill (broiler). Bring 170 ml (5½ fl oz/⅔ cup) water to the boil in a small saucepan, pour in couscous, then take the pan off the heat and leave it to stand for 10 minutes.

Heat the oil in a frying pan (skillet) and fry the onion and zucchini until lightly browned. Add capsicum and semi-dried tomatoes, then stir in the couscous. Stir in orange zest, one third of the orange juice and mint.

Put the chicken in a small shallow baking dish in a single layer and dot it with the butter. Sprinkle with the remaining orange juice and season with salt and pepper. Grill chicken for 8 to 10 minutes, turning it over halfway through. The skin should be browned and crisp.

Serve the chicken on the couscous with any juices poured over it.

Serves 1

Shepherd's pie

1 tablespoon oil
1 small onion, finely chopped
1 small carrot, finely chopped
250 g (9 oz) minced (ground) lamb, raw or cooked
plain (all-purpose) flour, for thickening
1 tablespoon tomato ketchup
½ a beef stock cube
worcestershire sauce, to taste
2 potatoes, peeled and cut into chunks
1 tablespoon milk
butter

Turn the oven on to 200°C (400°F/Gas 6). Heat the oil in a frying pan (skillet), add the onion and carrot and fry them together until they begin to brown around edges. Add meat and cook, turning over every now and then, mashing out any large lumps with the back of a fork.

When the meat is browned all over, add about half a teaspoon of flour, and stir it in. Add the ketchup and sprinkle on the stock cube. Now add 125 ml (4 fl oz/½ cup) of water and mix everything together. Bring mixture to the boil, then turn down heat and simmer gently for about 30 minutes, or until thick. Add a little more water if desired. Season with salt, pepper and worcestershire sauce.

While meat is cooking, cook potato chunks in simmering water until tender (this will take about 12 minutes). When soft, drain and mash them with milk and plenty of seasoning. Pour meat into a small ovenproof dish and dollop potato on top. Dot some butter over potato and bake for 20 minutes, by which time top of the potato should be lightly browned. Serve with peas.

Serves 1

Goan prawn curry

3 teaspoons oil
1 tablespoon curry paste
½ small onion, finely chopped
1 tomato, chopped
1 garlic clove, chopped
½ small green chilli, seeded and finely chopped
2 cm (½ inch) piece ginger, grated
1 tablespoon tamarind purée
60 ml (2 fl oz/¼ cup) coconut cream
5–6 prawns (shrimp), peeled and deveined

Heat oil in a small deep frying pan (skillet) or wok. Add curry paste, and fry for about a minute, by which time it should start to be aromatic. Add the onion and fry until golden. Add the tomato, garlic, green chilli and the ginger and fry over a low heat, stirring occasionally, for 8 minutes, or until the oil separates out from the sauce.

Add tamarind to the pan and bring everything to the boil. Add coconut cream and stir. Season with salt.

Add the prawns and bring everything slowly to the boil. (The sauce is not very liquidy, but it needs to be made very hot in order to cook the prawns.) Simmer the prawns for 3–5 minutes, or until they turn bright pink all over. Stir them around as they cook. Serve with rice or Indian breads.

Serves 1

Pulao with fried onions and spiced chicken

250 ml (9 fl oz/1 cup) chicken stock
1½ tablespoons oil
2 cardamom pods
2.5 cm (1 inch) piece cinnamon stick
1 clove
2 black peppercorns
95 g (3¼ oz/½ cup) basmati rice
2 tablespoons coriander (cilantro) leaves
1 small onion, finely sliced
1 teaspoon curry paste (any type)
2 teaspoons tomato paste (purée)
1 tablespoon plain yoghurt
1 boneless, skinless chicken breast, cut into strips
thick Greek-style yoghurt, to serve
mango chutney, to serve

Heat the chicken stock in a small saucepan until it is simmering. In a seperate saucepan heat 1 teaspoon of oil over medium heat. Add the cardamom pods, the cinnamon stick, clove and peppercorns and fry for a minute. Reduce heat to low, add the rice and stir constantly for 1 minute. Add heated stock and some salt to the rice and quickly bring everything to the boil. Cover the saucepan and simmer the rice over a low heat for 15 minutes. Leave rice to stand for 10 minutes, then stir in the coriander.

Heat 1 tablespoon of oil in a small frying-pan (skillet) and fry the onion until very soft. Increase the heat and keep frying until the onion turns dark brown. Drain onion on paper towels, then add to rice.

Mix curry paste, tomato paste and yoghurt together, then mix the paste thoroughly with the chicken strips.

Heat remaining oil in pan. Cook the chicken for 4 minutes over a high heat until almost black in patches.

Serve the rice with the chicken strips, yoghurt and mango chutney.

Serves1

Roast chicken pieces with herbed cheese

2 tablespoons herbed cream cheese
½ teaspoon grated lemon zest
1 whole chicken leg (Marylands) or breast, skin on
1 leek, cut into chunks
1 parsnip, peeled and cut into chunks
1 teaspoon olive oil

Preheat oven to 200°C (400°F/Gas 6). Mix cream cheese with lemon zest. Loosen the skin from the whole leg or chicken breast and spread the cream cheese between skin and flesh. Press the skin back down and season it.

Bring a saucepan of water to the boil and cook the leek and parsnip for 4 minutes. Drain well and put them in a single layer in a small baking dish. Drizzle with the oil and season well. Put the chicken on top and put the dish in the oven.

Roast for 40 minutes, by which time the skin should be browned and the cream cheese should have mostly melted out to form a sauce over the vegetables. Check that the vegetables are cooked and tender by prodding them with a knife. If they need a little longer, cover dish with foil and cook for another 5 minutes. Keep chicken warm under foil in the meantime.

Serves 1

Farfalle with prawns and lemon horseradish cream

100 g (3½ oz) farfalle pasta
2 teaspoons olive oil
1 French shallot, sliced
5–6 tiger prawns (shrimp), peeled and deveined
1 tablespoon lemon juice
3 tablespoons pouring cream
1 teaspoon grated lemon zest
1 tablespoon horseradish cream
1 tablespoon chervil leaves

Cook farfalle in a saucepan of boiling salted water until al dente, stirring once or twice to make sure the pieces are not stuck together. The cooking time will vary depending on the brand of pasta. Check the pasta occasionally as it cooks because the time given on packet instructions is often too long by a minute or two.

Heat the oil in a small frying pan (skillet) and add shallot. Cook for a minute, then add the prawns. Cook over a high heat for 2 or 3 minutes, or until prawns have turned bright pink and are cooked through. Add lemon juice and toss well. Turn off heat and leave everything in the pan.

Put cream in a small glass bowl and whisk it until it just starts to thicken. Don't make it too thick because when you add lemon zest and the lemony prawns the acid will thicken it further. Fold lemon zest, horseradish cream and chervil into the cream.

Drain farfalle and tip it back into the saucepan. Add the prawns and lemon juice to a bowl and the cream mixture. Fold everything together and season with salt and pepper. Pile into a deep serving bowl and serve immediately.

Serves 1

Spaghetti bolognese

1 tablespoon olive oil
1 garlic clove, crushed
1 small onion, chopped
1 small carrot, finely chopped
1 celery stalk, finely chopped
250 g (9 oz) lean minced (ground) beef
250 ml (9 fl oz/1 cup) beef stock
185 ml (6 fl oz/¾ cup) red wine
400 g (14 oz) tin chopped tomatoes
½ teaspoon sugar
2 tablespoons finely chopped parsley
100 g (3½ oz) spaghetti
grated parmesan cheese, to serve

Note: Reheat leftover meat sauce in the microwave. It will keep covered and refrigerated for 2 days. Freeze the remaining meat sauce in an airtight container. Defrost as needed and serve with freshly cooked pasta and parmesan cheese.

Heat some olive oil in a deep frying pan (skillet), then add garlic, onion, carrot and celery and stir over low heat for 5 minutes until vegetables are just starting to become tender.

Increase heat before adding the beef. You'll need to stir the meat to break up any lumps — a wooden spoon is good for this. Once the meat is nicely browned, add the stock, wine, tomatoes, sugar and parsley. Bring to the boil, then reduce the heat and simmer for 1 hour or thereabouts, stirring occasionally. Season with salt and freshly ground black pepper.

To make a single serve, and shortly before serving, cook the spaghetti in a saucepan of boiling, salted water until al dente. Drain and serve with half the meat sauce and sprinkle with some of the parmesan cheese.

Makes 2 serves/portions

Spicy eggplant spaghetti

100 g (3½ oz) spaghetti
2 tablespoons extra virgin olive oil
½ small red chilli, seeded and finely sliced
1 small onion, finely chopped
1 garlic clove, crushed
1 bacon slice, rind removed and chopped
100 g (3½ oz) eggplant (aubergine), diced
2 teaspoons balsamic vinegar
1 tomato, chopped
2 tablespoons shredded basil

Cook the pasta in a large pan of rapidly boiling water until al dente, then drain.

Heat 1 tablespoon of the oil in a deep frying pan (skillet) and cook the chilli, onion, garlic and bacon over medium heat for 5 minutes, or until the onion is golden and the bacon browned. Remove from the pan with a slotted spoon and set aside.

Add the remaining tablespoon of oil to pan and cook eggplant over high heat, tossing to brown on all sides. Return bacon mixture to pan, add vinegar, tomato and basil and cook until heated through. Season well.

Serve the spaghetti topped with the eggplant mixture.

Serves 1

Red beans and rice

105 g (3½ oz/½ cup) red kidney beans
1 tablespoon oil
1 small onion, finely chopped
1 small green capsicum (pepper), chopped
1 celery stalk, finely chopped
1 garlic clove, crushed
115 g (4 oz) andouille or other spicy sausage, cut into pieces
1 small or half a ham hock
1 bay leaf
100 g (3½ oz/½ cup) long-grain rice
2 spring onions (scallions), finely sliced, to garnish

Soak the red kidney beans overnight in cold water. Drain and put into a saucepan with enough cold water to cover the beans. Bring to the boil, then reduce the heat to a simmer.

Heat oil in a small frying pan (skillet) and sauté the onion, capsicum, celery and garlic until soft. Add sausage and sauté until it begins to brown around the edges.

Add sautéed vegetables and sausage to the beans in saucepan, along with ham and bay leaf. Bring to the boil, then reduce to a simmer and cook for 2½–3 hours, adding more water if necessary — beans should be saucy but not too liquidy. When the beans are almost cooked, boil the rice in a separate saucepan until tender.

To make one serve, top a portion of the cooked rice with some red kidney beans. Tear meat off the ham hock and add to the serving plate. Garnish with the sliced spring onion.

Makes 2 serves/portions

Note: Keep leftover beans and rice covered and refrigerated for up to 2 days. Gently reheat or microwave as needed. Suitable to freeze.

Spaghetti with meatballs

Meatballs
250 g (9 oz) minced (ground) beef
20 g (¾ oz/¼ cup) fresh breadcrumbs
1 small onion, finely chopped
1 garlic clove, crushed
1 teaspoon worcestershire sauce
½ teaspoon dried oregano
plain (all-purpose) flour, for dusting
2 tablespoons olive oil

Sauce
400 g (14 oz) tin chopped tomatoes
2 teaspoons olive oil
1 small onion, finely chopped
1 garlic clove, crushed
1 tablespoon tomato paste (purée)
60 ml (2 fl oz/¼ cup) beef stock
1 teaspoon sugar

100 g (3½ oz) spaghetti
grated parmesan cheese, optional

Note: Cover and refrigerate leftover meatballs and sauce. Reheat gently and then serve with freshly cooked spaghetti, or rice if you prefer. This dish can also be kept frozen for up to 1 month in portion-sized containers.

Combine the mince, breadcrumbs, onion, garlic, worcestershire sauce and oregano in a bowl and season to taste. Use your hands to mix the ingredients together well. Roll level tablespoons of the mixture into balls, dust lightly with flour and shake off excess. Heat oil in a deep frying-pan (skillet) and cook meatballs in batches, turning frequently, until browned all over. Drain well on paper towels.

To make sauce, purée tomatoes in a food processor or blender. Heat oil in the cleaned frying pan (skillet). Add onion and cook over medium heat for a few minutes until soft and just golden. Add the garlic and cook for 1 minute more. Add the puréed tomatoes, tomato paste, stock and sugar to the pan and stir to combine. Bring the mixture to the boil, and add meatballs. Reduce heat and simmer for 15 minutes, turning the meatballs once. Season with salt and pepper.

Meanwhile, for a single serving, cook the spaghetti in a large pan of boiling water until just tender. Drain, put into a deep serving plate and top with a portion of the meatballs and sauce. Serve with grated parmesan if desired.

Makes 2 serves/portions

Snapper pie

2 teaspoons olive oil
1 small onion, thinly sliced
125 ml (4 fl oz/½ cup) fish stock
250 ml (9 fl oz/1 cup) pouring cream
125 g (4½ oz) skinless and boneless snapper fillet, cut into large pieces
1 sheet puff pastry, thawed
1 egg, lightly beaten

Preheat the oven to 220°C (425°F/Gas 7). Heat the oil in a small frying pan (skillet), add onion and stir over a medium heat for 15 minutes, or until the onion is slightly caramelised. Add fish stock, bring to the boil and cook for 5 minutes, or until liquid is nearly evaporated. Stir in cream and bring to the boil. Reduce heat and simmer for 15 minutes, or until the liquid is reduced by half.

Put half the sauce into a 500 ml (17 fl oz/2 cup) capacity ramekin. Place the fish pieces into ramekin and top with remaining sauce. Cut pastry sheet slightly larger than the top of the ramekin. Brush edges of pastry with a little more of the egg, press pastry onto ramekin and brush the top with more beaten egg. Prick top and make a decorative cut out with remaining pastry. Bake for 30 minutes, or until well puffed.

Serves 1

Osso buco with gremolata

1 tablespoon olive oil
1 small onion, finely chopped
1 garlic clove, crushed
500 (1 lb 2 oz) veal shin slices (osso buco)
1 tablespoon plain (all-purpose) flour
200 g (7 oz) tinned tomatoes, roughly chopped
125 ml (4 fl oz/½ cup) white wine
125 ml (4 fl oz/½ cup) chicken stock

Gremolata
1 tablespoon finely chopped parsley
1 teaspoon grated lemon zest
1 small garlic clove, finely chopped

Note: Try to make this dish a day in advance as the flavours will improve considerably. Cover and refrigerate the remaining osso buco and reheat when needed. It will keep, refrigerated for up to 3 days, or frozen in an airtight container.

Heat half of the oil in a shallow flameproof casserole dish. Add onion and cook over low heat until soft and golden. Add garlic. Cook for 1 minute, then remove from the dish.

Heat remaining oil and brown the veal, then remove. Return the onion to the casserole and stir in the flour. Cook for 30 seconds and remove from heat. Slowly stir in the tomatoes, wine and stock, combining well with the flour. Return the veal to the casserole.

Return to the heat and bring to the boil, stirring. Cover and reduce the heat to low so that the casserole is just simmering. Cook for 2 hours, or until the meat is very tender and almost falling off the bones.

To make the gremolata, combine parsley, lemon zest and garlic in a bowl. When the osso buco is ready, spoon a portion onto a plate and sprinkle the gremolata over the top and serve with risotto or plain rice.

Makes 2 serves/portions

Asian chicken noodle soup

1 dried Chinese mushroom
60 g (2¼ oz) thin dry egg noodles
2 teaspoons oil
1 spring onion (scallion), julienned
2 teaspoons soy sauce
1 tablespoon rice wine, mirin or sherry
420 ml (14½ fl oz/1⅔ cups) chicken stock
1 small cooked chicken breast, shredded
1 small slice ham, cut into strips
a handful of bean sprouts
coriander (cilantro) leaves and thinly sliced red chilli, to garnish

Soak the mushroom in boiling water for 10 minutes to soften. Squeeze dry then remove the tough stem from the mushroom and slice thinly.

Cook noodles in a large pan of boiling water for 3 minutes, or according to the manufacturer's directions. Drain and cut noodles into shorter lengths with scissors.

Heat the oil in a heavy-based pan. Add the mushroom and spring onion. Cook for 1 minute, then add the soy sauce, the rice wine and the stock. Bring slowly to the boil and cook for 1 minute. Reduce heat and add noodles, shredded chicken, ham and the bean sprouts. Heat through for 2 minutes without allowing to boil.

Put noodles into a deep serving bowl, ladle in remaining mixture, and garnish with coriander leaves and sliced chilli.

Serves 1

Genovese pesto sauce

Pesto
2 garlic cloves
50 g (1¾ oz/⅓ cup) pine nuts
120 g (4½ oz/1 bunch) basil, stems removed
150–180 ml (5–6 fl oz) extra virgin olive oil
50 g (1¾ oz/½ cup) parmesan cheese, finely grated, plus extra to serve

100 g (3½ oz) trenette pasta
50 g (1¾ oz) green beans, trimmed
50 g (1¾ oz) small potatoes, very thinly sliced

Put the garlic and pine nuts in a mortar and pestle or food processor and pound or process until finely ground. Add the basil and then drizzle in the olive oil a little at a time while pounding or processing. When you have a thick purée stop adding the oil. Season and mix in the parmesan. Put the pesto into a jar, cover with a thin layer of oil, seal and refrigerate. It will keep for 1 month.

For a single serve, bring a saucepan of salted water to the boil. Add the pasta, green beans and potatoes, stirring well to prevent the pasta from sticking together. Cook until the pasta is al dente (the vegetables should be cooked by this time), then drain, reserving a little of the water.

Return pasta and vegetables to the saucepan, add a good dollop or two of pesto, and mix well. If necessary, add some of the reserved water to loosen the pasta. Season and serve immediately with the extra parmesan.

Serves 1

Prawn pulao

95 g (3¼ oz/½ cup) basmati rice
100 g (3½ oz) small prawns (shrimp)
1 tablespoon oil
1 small onion, finely chopped
¼ piece of cinnamon stick
2 cardamom pods
2 cloves
1 small stalk lemongrass, finely chopped
2 garlic cloves, crushed
2.5 cm (1 inch) piece of fresh ginger, grated
⅛ teaspoon ground turmeric

Wash the rice under cold running water and drain. Peel and devein prawns, then wash and pat dry with paper towels.

Heat oil in a deep frying pan (skillet) over a low heat and fry onion, spices and lemongrass. Stir in garlic, ginger and turmeric. Add the prawns and stir until pink. Toss in the rice and fry for 2 minutes.

Pour in 250 ml (9 fl oz/1 cup) of boiling water and add a pinch of salt. Bring to the boil. Reduce the heat and simmer for 15 minutes. Remove from the heat, cover and stand for 10 minutes. Fluff up the rice before serving.

Serves 1

Spicy Portuguese chicken soup

- 375 ml (13 fl oz/1½ cups) chicken stock
- ½ small onion, cut into thin wedges
- ½ small celery stalk, finely chopped
- ½ teaspoon grated lemon zest
- 1 tomato, peeled, seeded and chopped
- 1 small sprig mint
- 1 small chicken breast
- 2 tablespoons long-grain rice
- 1-2 teaspoons lemon juice
- 1 tablespoon shredded mint leaves

Combine the chicken stock, onion, celery, lemon zest, tomato and mint in a saucepan. Slowly bring to the boil, then reduce heat, add chicken breast and simmer gently for 15–20 minutes, or until the chicken is cooked through.

Remove chicken from the saucepan and discard the mint sprig. Allow to cool, then thinly slice.

Meanwhile, add rice to the pan and simmer for 20–25 minutes, or until tender. Return sliced chicken to pan, add lemon juice to taste and stir for 1–2 minutes, or until the chicken is warmed through. Season with salt and pepper, and stir through the mint.

Serves 1

Spiced eggplant

1 eggplant (aubergine), sliced into about eight 1 cm (½ inch) slices
250 g (9 oz/1 cup) tinned chopped tomatoes
1 small onion, finely chopped
2 cm (¾ inch) piece fresh ginger, grated
2 garlic cloves, crushed
1 small red chilli, seeded and finely chopped
oil, for frying
¼ teaspoon ground turmeric
¼ teaspoon nigella seeds (kalonji)
1 teaspoon garam masala
a small handful coriander (cilantro), chopped

Note: Cover and refrigerate leftover eggplant for up to 4 days. Reheat gently or have at room temperature. To reduce amount of oil used, brush eggplant slices with oil and grill for 5 minutes, turning once, until tender.

Put the eggplant slices in a colander. Sprinkle with salt; leave 30 minutes. Rinse slices and squeeze them to get rid of any excess water, then pat dry with paper towels.

Put tomatoes in a bowl then mix in onion, ginger, garlic and chilli. Heat a little oil in a deep, heavy-based frying pan (skillet) and, when hot, add as many eggplant slices as you can fit in a single layer. Cook them over a medium heat until browned on both sides, then drain them on paper towels to get rid of any excess oil. Cook the rest of the eggplant in batches, using as much oil as you need and draining off the excess.

Heat 2 teaspoons of oil in the frying pan, add the turmeric, nigella seeds and the garam masala and stir for a few seconds, then add the tomato mixture. Cook, stirring, for 5 minutes, or until mixture thickens. Carefully add the cooked eggplant so the slices stay whole. Cover pan and cook gently for about 15 minutes. Season with salt to taste and scatter with coriander. Serve 3 or 4 eggplant slices and some sauce for a single serve.

Makes 2 serves/portions

Fajitas

1½ tablespoons olive oil
1 tablespoon lime juice
1 garlic clove, chopped
¼ red chilli, seeded and chopped
2 teaspoons tequila (optional)
125 g (4½ oz) rump steak, thinly sliced into strips
½ small red and yellow capsicum (pepper), thinly sliced
½ small red onion, thinly sliced
2 flour tortillas
guacamole
shredded lettuce
diced tomato
sour cream

First make a marinade out of the oil, lime juice, garlic, chilli, tequila and some pepper. Add meat, cover and marinate in the refrigerator for several hours or overnight, if you have time.

Drain meat and toss it with capsicum and onion. Around the time that you want to eat, wrap the tortillas in foil and warm them in a 150°C (300°F/Gas 2) oven for 5 minutes. Cook the meat and vegetables in batches in a sizzling hot heavy-based frying pan (skillet) until cooked, then scoop onto the tortillas.

Assemble the fajitas, topped with the guacamole, shredded lettuce, diced tomato and the sour cream.

Serves 1

Ham and pea soup

1 tablespoon olive oil
1 small onion, chopped
1 celery stalk, sliced
about 8 sage leaves
110 g (3¾ oz/½ cup) green split peas, rinsed and drained
1 small or half a smoked ham hock, about 400 g (14 oz)
1 thyme sprig
vegetable oil, for pan-frying

Note: Smoked ham hocks are available from butchers and some delicatessens. The soup will keep in the refrigerator, covered, for up to 4 days, or put into portion-sized airtight containers in the freezer for up to 1 month

Heat oil in a saucepan over medium heat. Add onion, celery and the sage leaves and fry, stirring often, for about 5 minutes, or until onion and celery are soft. Remove half the sage leaves and set aside.

Add the green split peas, ham hock, thyme sprig and 750 ml (26 fl oz/ 3 cups) of water. Bring to the boil, then reduce heat, cover and simmer for 1½ hours, or until meat is falling off the bone.

Remove saucepan from the heat and discard the thyme sprig. Remove the ham hock from the saucepan and, when cool enough to handle, cut off meat and return it to soup. Discard the bone. Using an immersion blender fitted with a chopping blade, whizz the soup for 30 seconds, or until smooth. Or mash all ingredients together and add in the chopped ham. Season with freshly ground black pepper, and salt if necessary – the ham may be quite salty already.

For one serve, gently reheat soup and ladle into a deep bowl. Sprinkle the reserved sage leaves on top of the soup. Serve with crusty bread.

Makes about 1.5 litre (52 fl oz/6 cups)

Potato gnocchi with gorgonzola, goat's cheese and thyme sauce

1 tablespoon roasted skinned hazelnuts
35 g (1¼ oz) gorgonzola cheese or other strong dry blue cheese
25 g (1 oz) goat's cheese
1 tablespoon fresh thyme leaves
½ teaspoon grated lemon zest
185 g (6½ oz) potato gnocchi
1 tablespoon extra virgin olive oil
1 small leek, white part only, thinly sliced
2 tablespoons pouring cream

Put hazelnuts in a mini processor and whizz in 2-second bursts for 20 seconds, or until roughly chopped. Transfer to a small bowl.

Put the goat's cheese, thyme, lemon zest and gorgonzola or blue cheese, in the mini processor and whizz in short bursts for 15 seconds, or until crumbled. If you don't have a food processor chop the hazelnuts by hand and then mash together the cheeses, thyme and lemon zest in a small bowl.

Cook potato gnocchi in a saucepan of boiling salted water, according to the manufacturer's instructions. Drain the gnocchi, return to the pan and toss with a teaspoon of the oil.

Meanwhile, heat remaining oil in a small frying pan (skillet), add leek and sauté for 5–6 minutes, or until softened. Add the cream and cheese mixture and cook, stirring, over low heat for 3–5 minutes, or until cheese has melted.

Add the cheese sauce to the gnocchi and gently toss through. Season with salt and freshly ground black pepper, to taste. Spoon into a serving bowl, sprinkle with the chopped hazelnuts and serve immediately.

Serves 1

Creamy ratatouille with farfalle

120 g (4½ oz) baby eggplant (aubergine)
2 garlic cloves, crushed
1½ tablespoons olive oil
½ small red capsicum (pepper)
½ small green capsicum (pepper)
1 small onion, diced
125 g (4½ oz/½ cup) tinned chopped tomatoes
1 small zucchini (courgette), finely diced
2 teaspoons chopped thyme leaves
1 tablespoon chopped parsley
2 tablespoons red wine
1 teaspoon soft brown sugar
1 teaspoon tomato paste (purée)
1 small handful basil leaves, plus extra whole leaves, to serve
100 g (3½ oz) farfalle pasta
2 tablespoons cream (whipping)

Heat grill (broiler) to high. Cut ends off eggplant and slice flesh lengthways into 1 cm (½ inch) strips. Spread on a baking tray lined with foil. In a bowl, mix half the crushed garlic with half the oil and brush over eggplant. Grill, turning once, for about 3–5 minutes, or until golden brown, then remove.

Cut the capsicums into flat pieces and remove seeds and membranes. Cook, skin-side-up, under the hot grill until skin blackens and blisters. Leave to cool in a plastic bag, then peel away the skin and cut the flesh into strips.

Heat remaining oil in a frying pan (skillet). Add onion and remaining garlic and gently sauté for 3 minutes. Stir through grilled eggplant, tomato capsicum, zucchini, thyme, parsley, wine, sugar, tomato paste and the basil leaves. Season well. Simmer, uncovered, for 30 minutes, stirring occasionally. Add water if needed to keep moist. While the ratatouille is simmering, cook pasta in a saucepan of boiling salted water until al dente. Drain, keep warm.

Take the ratatouille off heat, add cream and stir through. Spoon the ratatouille sauce over top of pasta. Garnish with basil leaves and serve.

Serves 1

Beetroot and red capsicum soup

- 3 medium beetroot (beets) – about 300 g (10½ oz) without stems and leaves
- 1 tablespoon oil
- 1 small red onion, chopped
- 1 small celery stalk, chopped
- 1 garlic clove, chopped
- 1 small red capsicum (pepper), seeded and chopped
- 200 g (7 oz) tinned chopped tomatoes
- 2 teaspoons red wine vinegar
- sour cream, to serve
- finely snipped chives, to serve

Wearing protective gloves, peel the beetroot with a vegetable peeler and cut into 3 cm (1¼ inch) cube. Put the beetroot in a saucepan with 500 ml (17 fl oz/2 cups) of water. Slowly bring to the boil over medium–low heat, then reduce the heat and simmer for 25–30 minutes, or until the beetroot is tender when pierced with a fork. Remove about half a cup of beetroot cubes, dice finely and set aside.

Meanwhile, heat oil in a heavy-based saucepan over medium heat. Add the onion, celery, garlic and the capsicum and stir to coat vegetables in the oil. Reduce heat to low, cover and cook, stirring occasionally, for 10 minutes. Do not allow the vegetables to brown. Add chopped tomatoes and vinegar and simmer for 10 minutes.

Transfer tomato mixture to saucepan containing beetroot and remove the pan from heat. Using an immersion blender fitted with the chopping blade, whizz soup for 20–30 seconds, or until smooth. Season well with salt and freshly ground black pepper.

For a single serve, ladle a portion of soup into a warm bowl and top with sour cream, some of the reserved diced beetroot and the chives.

Makes 1.25 litres (44 fl oz/5 cups)

Note: The soup will keep in the refrigerator, covered, for up to 4 days, or put into portion-sized airtight containers in the freezer for up to 1 month. If you do not have an immersion blender, you can use a food processor or simply mash with a potato masher.

Spinach and lentil soup

60 g (2¼ oz/⅓ cup) green lentils, rinsed and picked over
500 ml (17 fl oz/2 cups) chicken stock
1 tablespoon olive oil
½ small onion, finely chopped
½ small fennel bulb, trimmed and finely diced
1 small carrot, finely diced
¼ teaspoon fennel seeds
pinch cayenne pepper
1 bay leaf
1 tablespoon tomato paste (concentrated purée)
1 garlic clove, halved lengthways and thinly sliced
1 handful baby English spinach, washed
small pinch of sweet smoked paprika
extra virgin olive oil, to serve

Put lentils in a small saucepan and cover with cold water. Bring to the boil over medium–high heat, reduce heat and simmer for 10 minutes. Drain and return to saucepan. Add the stock and bring to the boil. Reduce the heat to medium and simmer for 15 minutes.

Meanwhile, heat half the oil in a heavy-based frying pan (skillet). Add the onion, fennel, carrot, fennel seeds and the cayenne pepper. Lightly crush bay leaves and add to pan. Sauté over low heat for 5 minutes, or until onion is translucent. Stir through the tomato paste. Add onion mixture and simmer, partially covered, for 20 minutes, or until tender.

Gently heat remaining oil in frying pan (skillet) over low heat. Add garlic and half the spinach and cook, stirring, for 2–3 minutes, or until spinach has wilted. Add the paprika and spinach mixture to the soup and simmer for 2 minutes. Remove saucepan from heat and discard bay leaves. Transfer half the soup to a blender or small processor. Whizz for 30 seconds, or until smooth, then return to saucepan and add remaining spinach. Season.

For a single serve, ladle a portion into a serving bowl, drizzle with virgin olive oil and sprinkle with black pepper.

Makes about 1 litre (35 fl oz/4 cups)

Note: Cover and refrigerate leftover soup and eat within 3 days. It can also be frozen in portion-sized containers.

Penne with zucchini, ricotta and parmesan sauce

100 g (3½ oz) small penne pasta

Sauce
1 zucchini (courgette), chopped
1 garlic clove, chopped
¼ small red chilli, seeded and chopped
60 g (2¼ oz/¼ cup) ricotta cheese
60 ml (2 fl oz/¼ cup) pouring cream
1 teaspoon finely grated lemon zest
25 g (1 oz/¼ cup) grated parmesan cheese
a small handful basil, chopped
small basil leaves, to serve
parmesan cheese shavings, to serve

Note: Prepare the sauce just prior to serving. It is not suitable for freezing.

Cook the penne pasta in a large saucepan of boiling salted water according to the manufacturer's instructions. Drain the penne, reserving 60 ml (2 fl oz/¼ cup) the cooking water.

Meanwhile, to make sauce, put the zucchini, garlic and chilli in a small processor fitted with the metal blade and whizz in short bursts for about 30 seconds, or until finely chopped. Add the ricotta, cream, lemon zest, parmesan and the chopped basil, and season well with salt and freshly ground black pepper. Whizz for 20 seconds, or until smooth.

Pour sauce over the hot penne, adding enough of the reserved cooking water to make a coating consistency. Serve immediately, topped with small basil leaves and parmesan shavings.

Serves 1

Warm Mediterranean lamb salad

250 g (9 oz) lamb back strap or loin fillets
1½ tablespoons olive oil
1 small garlic clove, crushed
1 teaspoon thyme leaves
¼ teaspoon ground black pepper
1 small red capsicum (pepper)
2 small slender eggplants (aubergines), thickly sliced on the diagonal
2 teaspoons olive tapenade
2 semi-dried (sun-blushed) tomatoes, sliced
¼ Lebanese (short) cucumber, seeded and chopped
40 g (1½ oz) green beans, trimmed and blanched
40 g (1½ oz/¼ cup) Niçoise or Ligurian olives
a large handful of baby rocket (arugula) leaves

Dressing
1 small garlic clove, crushed
1 tablespoon extra virgin olive oil
2 teaspoons lemon juice

Note: Instead of chargrilling the red capsicum slices, you can purchase them already prepared.

Put the lamb in a non-metallic bowl. Combine half the oil with the garlic, thyme and pepper, then pour over the lamb and toss to coat. Set aside. Heat grill (broiler) to high. Cut the capsicum into large flat pieces, discarding the seeds and membrane. Arrange skin-side-up on grill tray and grill until the skin blackens and blisters. Leave to cool in a plastic bag, then peel away the skin and cut the flesh into thirds.

Meanwhile, preheat barbecue chargrill plate or chargrill pan to high. Toss the eggplant in the remaining oil to coat and grill for 2–3 minutes on each side, or until golden. Remove and drain on paper towels. Cook the lamb on the hot chargrill plate or pan for 4 minutes on each side for medium rare, or until done to your liking. Remove from the heat, cover loosely with foil and leave to rest for 5 minutes. Thinly slice the lamb across the grain and toss in a large bowl with capsicum, eggplant, tapenade, tomato, cucumber, beans and olives. Add the rocket.

Place dressing ingredients in a small screw-top jar; shake well. Pour over the lamb salad, season with salt and pepper and toss to combine.

Serves 1

Dinner

Twice-baked cheese soufflés

125 ml (4 fl oz/½ cup) milk
2 black peppercorns
small segment of onion, studded with 2 cloves
1 bay leaf
30 g (1 oz) butter
35 g (1¼ oz/¼ cup) self-raising flour
1 egg, separated
65 g (2¼ oz/½ cup) Gruyère cheese, grated
125 ml (4 fl oz/½ cup) pouring cream
25 g (1 oz/¼ cup) parmesan cheese, finely grated

Note: The remaining soufflé can be finished off the next day with the cream and parmesan.

Preheat the oven to 180°C (350°F/Gas 4). Lightly grease two 125 ml (4 fl oz/½ cup) ramekins. Place milk, peppercorns, onion and bay leaf in a small saucepan and heat until nearly boiling. Remove from the heat and let it infuse for 10 minutes. Strain.

Melt butter in a small saucepan, add flour and cook over a medium heat for 1 minute. Remove from heat and gradually stir in the infused milk, then return to the heat and stir until the mixture boils and thickens. Simmer for 1 minute.

Transfer the mixture to a bowl and add the egg yolk and gruyère cheese. Beat egg white until soft peaks form, then gently fold into the cheese sauce. Divide mixture between the ramekins and place in a baking dish half-filled with hot water. Bake for 15 minutes. Remove from the baking dish, cool and refrigerate.

Preheat the oven to 200°C (400°F/Gas 6). For one serve, remove one of the soufflés from a ramekin and place onto an ovenproof plate. Pour half the cream over top and sprinkle with half the parmesan. Bake for 20 minutes, or until puffed and golden. Serve with a salad.

Makes 2

Coq au vin

2 teaspoons olive oil
4 white baby onions, peeled
1 rindless bacon slice, chopped
20 g (¾ oz) butter
500 g (1 lb 2 oz) chicken pieces
1 garlic clove, crushed
125 ml (4 fl oz/½ cup) dry red wine
1 tablespoon brandy
2 teaspoons chopped thyme
1 bay leaf
1 parsley stalk
85 g (3 oz) button mushrooms, halved
2 teaspoons butter, extra, softened
2 teaspoons plain (all-purpose) flour
chopped parsley, to serve

Note: Cover and refrigerate remaining coq au vin. It will keep for 3 days. Gently reheat before serving. It can also be frozen in an airtight container for up to 1 month.

Preheat oven to warm 170°C (325°F/ Gas 3). Heat the oil in a heavy-based frying pan (skillet) and add the onions. Cook until browned, then add bacon and cook until browned. Remove bacon and onions and add butter to the pan. When the butter is foaming add the chicken in a single layer and cook in batches until well browned. Transfer chicken to an ovenproof dish, draining it of any fat, then add the onions and bacon.

Tip any excess fat out of the frying pan and add the garlic, wine, brandy, thyme, bay leaf and the parsley stalk. Bring to the boil and pour over the chicken. Cook, covered, in the oven for 1 hour and 25 minutes, then add mushrooms and cook for 30 minutes. Drain through a colander and reserve the liquid in a pan. Keep the chicken warm in the oven.

Mix softened butter and flour together, bring the liquid in the pan to the boil and whisk in the flour and butter paste in two batches, then reduce heat and simmer until the liquid thickens slightly. Remove the parsley stalk and bay leaf from the chicken and return it to the ovenproof dish. Pour in the sauce, scatter on the chopped parsley. For one serve spoon out a portion onto a plate and serve.

Makes 2 serves/portions

Pepper steak

200 g (7 oz) fillet steak
2 teaspoons oil
1 tablespoon black peppercorns, crushed
20 g (¾ oz) butter
1 tablespoon Cognac or brandy
1 tablespoon white wine
2 tablespoons thick (double/heavy) cream
green salad, to serve

Rub steak on both sides with the oil and press crushed peppercorns into the meat so they don't come off while you're frying. Melt the butter in a small frying pan (skillet) and cook the steak for 2–4 minutes on each side, depending on how you like your steak.

Now for the fun part: add Cognac or brandy and flambé by lighting the pan with your gas flame or a match (stand well back when you do this and keep a pan lid handy for emergencies). Lift steak out onto a warm serving plate. Add wine to the pan and boil, stirring, for 1 minute to deglaze the pan. Add cream and stir for a couple of minutes. Season with salt and pepper and pour over steak. Serve with green salad.

Serves 1

Teppanyaki

85 g (3 oz) piece fillet steak
assorted vegetables, such as green beans, slender eggplant (aubergine), shiitake mushrooms, red or green capsicum (pepper), spring onions (scallions)
3 prawns (shrimp), peeled and deveined, with tails intact
oil, for frying
soy sauce

First, you need to slice the meat very thinly. The secret to this is to partially freeze the meat (about 30 minutes should be enough), then slice it with a very sharp knife. Place meat slices in a single layer on a large serving platter and season well with salt and pepper.

Cut vegetables into long, thin strips, then arrange them in separate bundles on a plate. Arrange the prawns on a third plate.

The idea with teppanyaki is to cook the meal at the table on a very hot electric grill (griddle) or frying pan (skillet). Lightly brush the pan with oil. Quickly fry the meat, searing on both sides, and then push it over to the edge of the pan while you cook the vegetables and the prawns. Serve with rice and soy sauce for dipping.

Serves 1

Steak with green peppercorn sauce

200 g (7 oz) fillet steak
1 teaspoon butter
½ teaspoon oil
60 ml (2 fl oz/¼ cup) beef stock
2 tablespoons cream
½ teaspoon cornflour (cornstarch)
2 teaspoons green peppercorns in brine, rinsed and drained
2 teaspoons brandy
potato chips, to serve
rosemary, to garnish

First of all, bash the steak with a meat mallet to 1.5 cm (⅝ inch) thick. Next, nick the edges of the steak to prevent it from curling when it is cooking.

Heat butter and oil in a small, heavy-based frying pan (skillet) over high heat. Fry the steak for 2–4 minutes on each side, depending on how you like it. Transfer to a serving plate and cover with foil.

Now add the stock to the pan juices and stir over low heat until boiling. Combine cream and cornflour, then pour the mixture into the pan and stir constantly until the sauce becomes smooth and thick — a few minutes will do the trick. Add peppercorns and brandy and boil for 1 minute before taking the pan off the heat. Spoon the sauce over the steak and serve with potato chips. Garnish with rosemary.

Serves 1

Pork chops pizzaiola

1 pork chop
1 tablespoon olive oil
2 ripe tomatoes
1 garlic clove, crushed
1 basil leaf, torn into pieces
1 teaspoon finely chopped parsley, to serve

Using scissors or a knife, cut the pork fat at 5 mm (¼ inch) intervals around the rind. Brush chop with 1 teaspoon of olive oil and season well.

Remove stems from the tomatoes and score a cross in the bottom of each one. Blanch in boiling water for 30 seconds. Transfer to cold water, peel skin away from the cross and chop the tomatoes.

Heat 2 teaspoons of oil in a saucepan over low heat and add garlic. Soften without browning for 1–2 minutes, then add tomato and season. Increase the heat, bring to the boil and cook for 5 minutes until thick. Stir in the basil.

Heat remaining oil in a small frying pan (skillet) with a tight-fitting lid. Brown chop over medium-high heat for 2 minutes on each side. Spoon the sauce over the top, covering the chop completely. Cover pan and cook over low heat for about 5 minutes. Sprinkle with parsley and serve with English spinach, if desired.

Serves 1

Braised sausages with Puy lentils

2 teaspoons olive oil
30 g (1 oz) pancetta, cubed
1 small red onion, finely chopped
2–3 Toulouse or pork sausages
1 garlic clove, peeled and smashed
1 sprig thyme leaves
70 g (2½ oz/⅓ cup) Puy lentils
185 ml (6 fl oz/¾ cup) tinned chicken consommé or chicken stock
2 large handfuls baby English spinach leaves, finely chopped
1 tablespoon crème fraîche

Heat oil in a heavy-based, lidded frying pan (skillet) and fry the pancetta until it is browned. Take it out using a slotted spoon, and put it in a bowl. Put onion in the pan and cook until it is soft and only lightly browned. Take the onion out, using a slotted spoon, and add it to pancetta. Put sausages in the same pan and fry until they are very brown all over. Put the pancetta and onion back in with the sausages.

Add the garlic and the thyme leaves to the frying pan, along with the lentils, and mix everything together. Add the consommé or stock and bring to the boil. Put a lid on frying pan and slowly simmer the mixture for 25–30 minutes, or until lentils are tender. Stir the spinach through.

Season the lentils with salt and pepper and stir in the crème fraîche. Serve the sausages with the lentils in a shallow bowl. Serve with bread.

Serves 1

Salmon nori roll with sesame noodles

85 g (3 oz) soba noodles
1 teaspoon sesame oil
2 teaspoons sesame seeds
1 piece salmon fillet (10 x 15 cm/ 4 x 6 inches), bones removed
1 sheet nori
2 teaspoons butter
2 large handfuls baby English spinach leaves

Cook noodles in a saucepan of boiling salted water for about 5 minutes, or until just cooked. The cooking time will vary depending on brand of noodles. Drain noodles, add the sesame oil and some seasoning, then toss them so they are coated in oil. Dry-fry sesame seeds in a frying pan (skillet) until they start to colour and smell toasted, then add to the noodles. Cover and keep warm.

Cut the salmon fillet in half horizontally and neaten edges. Cut sheet of nori in half with scissors and lay a piece of salmon fillet on top of each half. Season well, then roll up the fillets to make two neat log shapes. Trim off any bits of nori or salmon that stick out. Using a sharp knife, cut each roll into three pieces.

Heat butter in a small non-stick frying pan and fry the pieces of roll until they are golden on each side and almost cooked all the way through. This will take about 4 minutes on each side. Lift out rolls. Add spinach to pan, stir it around until it wilts, then turn off the heat. Serve salmon with noodles and some spinach on the side.

Serves 1

Grilled trout with lemon butter and couscous

60 g (2¼ oz/⅓ cup) instant couscous
2 teaspoons olive oil
1 small onion, finely chopped
1 piece of red or yellow chargrilled capsicum (pepper), chopped
a small handful pine nuts
lemon juice and zest from ½ a lemon
a small handful mint, chopped
1 rainbow trout fillet, with the skin removed
2 teaspoons butter, softened

Heat the grill (broiler). Bring 170 ml (5½ fl oz/⅔ cup) water to the boil in a saucepan and pour in the couscous. Take the pan off the heat and leave it to stand for 10 minutes.

Heat the oil in a frying pan (skillet) and fry the onion until it is lightly browned. Add capsicum and pine nuts, then stir in the couscous. Stir through half of the lemon juice and zest and the mint.

Put the trout fillet on an oiled baking tray. Mix butter with the rest of the lemon zest and spread on to the fish. Grill the fish for 6 minutes, or until just cooked through. Sprinkle on the rest of the lemon juice and season well.

Serve trout (take it off the tray carefully as it hasn't got any skin to help hold it together) on the couscous with any buttery juices poured over it.

Serves 1

Lamb cutlets with onion and herb marmalade

Marmalade
1 tablespoon butter
2 tablespoons olive oil
2 small onions, finely sliced
1 teaspoon brown sugar
1 teaspoon thyme leaves
1 tablespoon finely chopped parsley
3–4 French-trimmed lamb cutlets
1 tablespoon lemon juice

Note: Covered and refrigerated, leftover marmalade will keep for a week.

For marmalade, heat the butter and olive oil together in a small saucepan. Add the onion, sugar and thyme and stir well. Turn heat to low, cover the saucepan and cook the onion, stirring it occasionally for 30 to 35 minutes, or until it is very soft and golden. Season well, stir the parsley through and keep it warm over a very low heat.

Heat a frying pan (skillet) or brush a griddle with a little extra oil and, when it is hot, add cutlets in a single layer. Fry for 2 minutes on each side, or until the lamb is browned on outside but still feels springy when you press it. Add the lemon juice and season well.

Put a small pile of the onion and herb marmalade on a serving plate and place the cutlets and any juices around it.

Serves 1

Summer seafood marinara

- 80 g (2¾ oz) fresh saffron angel hair pasta
- 2 teaspoons extra virgin olive oil
- 1 tablespoon butter
- 1 garlic clove, finely chopped
- 1 small onion, finely chopped
- ½ small red chilli, seeded and finely chopped
- 150 g (5 oz) tinned chopped tomatoes
- 60 ml (2 fl oz/¼ cup) white wine
- zest of ½ a lemon
- 1 teaspoon sugar
- 50 g (1¾ oz) scallops without roe
- 125 g (4½ oz) raw prawns (shrimp), peeled and deveined
- 80 g (2¾ oz) clams (vongole)

Cook the pasta in a large saucepan of rapidly boiling water until al dente. Drain and keep warm.

Heat oil and butter in a large frying pan (skillet), add the garlic, onion and chilli and cook over a medium heat for 5 minutes, or until soft but not golden. Add tomatoes and wine and bring to the boil. Cook for about 10 minutes, or until sauce the has reduced and thickened slightly.

Add the lemon zest, sugar, scallops, prawns and clams and cook, covered, for 5 minutes, or until the seafood is tender. Discard any shells that do not open. Season with salt and pepper. Serve the sauce on top of the pasta.

Serves 1

Beef cooked in Guinness

1 tablespoon oil
500 g (1 lb 2 oz) chuck steak, cubed
1 onion, chopped
1 garlic clove, crushed
1 teaspoon brown sugar
1 teaspoon plain (all-purpose) flour
60 ml (2 fl oz/¼ cup) Guinness
185 ml (6 fl oz/¾ cup) beef stock
1 bay leaf
1 sprig thyme

1 slice baguette, toasted
½ teaspoon dijon mustard

Note: Freeze leftover beef casserole or reheat in a microwave the next day. It will keep for 2 days refrigerated. The flavour improves on keeping.

Put oven on to 180°C (350°F/Gas 4). Heat half the oil in a frying pan (skillet) over a high heat and fry the meat in batches until browned all over. Add more oil as required. Put meat in a casserole dish.

Add the onion to the frying pan and fry gently over a low heat. When the onion starts to brown, add the garlic and brown sugar and cook until the onion is fairly brown. Stir in flour, then transfer to the casserole dish.

Put Guinness and stock in the frying pan and bring it to the boil, then pour into the casserole dish. Add the bay leaf and thyme and season well. Bring to the boil, put a lid on and put the casserole in the oven for 2 hours.

Spread the bread with the mustard and serve a portion of the beef ladled over. Serve with celeriac or potato mash on the side.

Makes 2 serves/portions

Pork chop with apple and cider

2 teaspoons oil
1 small onion, sliced
1 small golden delicious apple, cored and cut into wedges
1 teaspoon caster (superfine) sugar
1 teaspoon butter
1 thick pork chop, snipped around the edges
2 tablespoons cider
2 tablespoons cream

Heat the oil in a non-stick frying pan (skillet), add onion and fry for about 5 minutes, or until soft and beginning to brown. Tip onion out onto a plate.

Add apple wedges to the pan and fry them for a minute or two — they should not break up, but should start to soften and brown. Add the sugar and butter and shake everything around in the pan until the apples start to caramelize. Transfer the apples to the plate with the onion.

Put pork chop in frying pan (skillet), add a bit of seasoning and fry for 4 minutes on each side, or until cooked through. Put the onion and the apple back in the pan and heat up, then add cider and bring to a simmer. Once liquid is bubbling, add cream and shake pan so everything mixes together. Let it bubble for a minute, then season well and serve with potatoes and a green salad — watercress goes particularly well.

Serves 1

Thai mussels with noodles

500 g (1 lb 2 oz) mussels
60 g (2¼ oz/1 small bundle) glass noodles
1 garlic clove, crushed
1 spring onion (scallion), finely chopped
1 tablespoon red curry paste
80 ml (2½ oz/⅓ cup) coconut cream
juice of 1 lime
1 tablespoon fish sauce
a small handful coriander (cilantro) leaves

Rinse the mussels in cold water and pull off any beards. Look at each one individually and, if it isn't tightly closed, tap it on the work surface to see if it will close. Throw away any mussels that won't close.

Soak the noodles in boiling water for a minute or two. Drain them and, using a pair of scissors, cut them into shorter lengths. Put the mussels in a deep frying pan (skillet) or wok with the garlic and spring onion and 60 ml (2 fl oz/¼ cup) water. Bring water to the boil, then put a lid on and cook mussels for 2 to 3 minutes, shaking occasionally, or until they are all open. Throw away any that don't open. Tip the whole lot, including any liquid, into a sieve lined with a piece of muslin (cheesecloth), over the bowl reserving the liquid.

Pour the cooking liquid back into the pan, add the curry paste, to taste and coconut cream and stir together. Bring mixture to the boil, then add lime juice and fish sauce. Put the mussels back in the pan. Cook for a minute, then stir in coriander leaves.

Put the noodles in a deep bowl and ladle the mussels and sauce on top.

Serves 1

Saltimbocca

2 small veal escalopes
2 slices prosciutto
2 sage leaves
1 tablespoon olive oil
30 g (1 oz) butter
60 ml (2 fl oz/¼ cup) dry Marsala or dry white wine

Place the veal between two sheets of baking paper and pound with a meat mallet or rolling pin until they are 5 mm (¼ in) thick. Make sure you pound them evenly. Peel off the paper and season lightly. Cut the prosciutto slices to the same size as the veal. Cover each piece of veal with a slice of prosciutto and place a sage leaf in the centre. Secure the sage leaf with a cocktail stick.

Heat olive oil and half the butter in a frying pan (skillet). Add veal and fry, prosciutto side up, over medium heat for 3–4 minutes, or until veal is just cooked through. Briefly flip saltimbocca over and fry prosciutto side. Transfer to a serving plate.

Pour off the oil from the pan and add the Marsala or wine. Bring to the boil and cook over high heat until reduced by half, scraping up the bits from the bottom of the pan. Add the remaining butter and, when it has melted, season the sauce. Remove cocktail sticks and spoon the sauce over the veal to serve.

Serves 1

Steak with maître d'hôtel butter

1 tablespoon unsalted butter, softened
1 teaspoon finely chopped parsley
few drops of lemon juice
1 steak, about 1.5 cm (¾ inch) thick
1 teaspoon olive oil

Beat the butter to a cream in a small bowl, using a wooden spoon, then beat in a pinch of salt, a pinch of the pepper and parsley. Next add a few drops of lemon juice. Let the butter harden in the fridge a little, then form it into a small round by rolling it up in greaseproof paper. Put it into the fridge until you need it.

Season steak with salt and pepper on both sides. Heat the oil in a small frying pan (skillet) and, when it is very hot, add steak. Cook for 2 minutes on each side for rare, 3 minutes on each side for medium, and 4 minutes on each side for well done. Timings may vary depending on the thickness of your steak — if it is thin, give it a slightly shorter time and if thick, cook for a little longer.

Put butter on top of the steak. The heat of steak will melt butter. Serve with potatoes and vegetables or salad.

Serves 1

Barbecued steak filled with bocconcini and semi-dried tomato

1 New York style (boneless sirloin) steak
2 semi-dried (sun-blushed) tomatoes, chopped
2 small bocconcini (fresh baby mozzarella) cheese, chopped
1 small garlic clove, crushed
1 teaspoon finely chopped flat-leaf (Italian) parsley
oil, for brushing

Note: You can fill the steak ahead of time — simply keep covered in the refrigerator. Bring to room temperature just before you're ready to cook.

Cut a slit along the side of the steak to form a pocket. Combine tomato, bocconcini, garlic and the parsley in a bowl with a little salt and pepper. Fill steak with mixture and secure with toothpicks to hold filling in.

Preheat a barbecue grill plate or chargrill pan to medium. Just before cooking, brush steak lightly with oil and season with salt and pepper. Grill the steak for 3–4 minutes on each side for medium rare, or until cooked to your liking, turning only once. Remove the toothpicks and serve with vegetables or a salad.

Serves 1

Veal stack with mozzarella

- 2 tablespoons tomato passata (puréed tomatoes)
- 1 small garlic clove, crushed
- pinch sugar
- oil, for brushing
- 150 g (5½ oz) butterflied veal loin steak
- small handful baby rocket (arugula) leaves
- 1 slice chargrilled eggplant (aubergine)
- 2 tablespoons coarsely grated mozzarella cheese

Put passata, garlic and sugar in a small bowl. Season to taste and set aside. Heat grill (broiler) to high. Brush the veal steak with a little oil, season with salt and pepper, then grill on the hotplate for 3–5 minutes on each side, or until nicely browned and cooked to your liking. Remove from the heat.

Arrange the rocket, eggplant slice, passata mixture and mozzarella on top of each steak. Put the steak on the grill plate under the hot grill and cook for 1 minute, or until cheese is golden. Serve hot.

Serves 1

Sweets

Double chocolate brownies

80 g (2¾ oz) butter
40 g (1½ oz/⅓ cup) cocoa powder
145 g (4¾ oz/⅔ cup) caster (superfine) sugar
2 eggs
75 g (2½ oz/½ cup) plain (all-purpose) flour
½ teaspoon baking powder
100 g (3½ oz/½ cup) chocolate chips

Preheat the oven to 180°C (350°F/Gas 4). Brush your cake tin with oil or melted butter, put a piece of baking paper in the bottom.

Melt the butter in a saucepan. When it is ready, take it off the heat and stir in cocoa and sugar, followed by eggs.

Put a sieve over the saucepan and tip in the flour and baking powder, along with a pinch of salt. Sift everything into the saucepan, then mix it in. Make sure you don't have any pockets of flour. Stir in the chocolate chips.

Pour mixture into your tin and bake it for 30 minutes. If you have used a different sized tin, the cooking time may be shorter (bigger tin) or longer (smaller tin). You will know the brownies are cooked when you can poke a skewer or knife into the middle of them and it comes out clean. Remember, though, the chocolate chips may have melted and if the skewer hits one of those, it might look as if the mixture is still wet. Leave the slab to cool in the tin, then tip it out and cut it into brownie pieces.

Makes 12 small pieces

Note: Store brownies refrigerated in an airtight container. They will keep for 1 week. You can also freeze them for up to 1 month.

Choc-hazelnut puff pastry rolls

2 tablespoons choc-hazelnut spread
40 g (1½ oz/⅓ cup) icing (confectioners') sugar
1 sheet puff pastry, thawed
1 egg, lightly beaten
icing (confectioners') sugar, extra

Preheat the oven to 200°C (400°F/Gas 6). Combine the choc-hazelnut spread and icing sugar in a small bowl and roll into a 10 cm (4 in) long roll. Wrap the roll in plastic wrap and twist the ends to enclose. Refrigerate for 30 minutes. When firm, cut the roll into four even pieces. Roll each of the pieces in extra icing sugar.

Cut the sheet of puff pastry into four squares. Place a piece of the choc-hazelnut mixture roll onto each square of pastry and roll up to enclose. Pinch the ends; brush lightly with egg. Bake for 15 minutes, or until the pastry is golden. Cool slightly. Dust with icing sugar.

Makes 4

Note: Refrigerate leftover pastries in an airtight container for up to 3 days.

Nursery rice pudding

75 g (2½ oz/⅓ cup) arborio or short-grain rice
500 ml (17 fl oz/2 cups) milk
2 tablespoons caster (superfine) sugar
½ teaspoon natural vanilla extract
60 ml (2 fl oz/¼ cup) cream

Note: Cover and refrigerate leftover rice pudding. It will keep for 3 days. Reheat gently or microwave.

Rinse the rice in a colander until the water runs clear. Drain well and place in a small heavy-based pan with the milk, sugar and vanilla.

Bring to the boil while stirring, then reduce the heat to the lowest setting and cook for about 35 minutes, stirring frequently, until the rice is thick and creamy.

Remove the pan from the heat and leave to stand for 10 minutes. Stir in the cream. Spoon a portion into a serving bowl and serve warm with stewed fruit, if desired.

Serves 1

Variation: Add a cinnamon stick and a strip of lemon zest to the rice in place of vanilla extract. Or add a small sprig of washed lavender to the rice while it is cooking.

Zabaglione

2 egg yolks
1 tablespoon caster (superfine) sugar
2 tablespoons sweet Marsala
80 ml (2½ fl oz/⅓ cup) thick (double/heavy) cream

Whisk the egg yolks and sugar in a small heatproof bowl set over a small saucepan of simmering water. Make sure that the base of the bowl does not touch the water or the egg may overcook and stick. It is important that you whisk constantly to move the cooked mixture from the outside of the bowl to the centre.

When the mixture is tepid, add the Marsala and whisk for an additional 5 minutes, or until it has thickened enough to hold its shape when drizzled off the whisk into the bowl.

Whip cream until soft peaks form. Gently fold in egg yolk and Marsala mixture. Pour into a serving glass or bowl. Cover and refrigerate for about 3–4 hours before serving.

Serves 1

Trifle

1 slice of madeira (pound) cake or trifle sponge
3 teaspoons sweet sherry or Madeira
a handful of raspberries
125 ml (4 fl oz/½ cup) bought vanilla custard
2 tablespoons thick (double/heavy) cream
1 tablespoon flaked almonds, to decorate
extra raspberries, to decorate

Put a slice of cake in the base of a serving bowl, then sprinkle it with the sherry. Scatter the raspberries over the top and crush them gently into the sponge with the back of a spoon to release their tart flavour, leaving some of them whole.

Pour the custard over the cake and raspberries and leave to set in the fridge — it will firm up but not become solid. Spoon cream over the custard. Go wild decorating with almonds and raspberries (or anything else you fancy) and refrigerate until needed.

Serves 1

Creamy chocolate mousse

30 g (1 oz) good-quality dark chocolate, chopped
1 egg, separated
2½ tablespoons cream, lightly whipped
cocoa powder, to serve

Melt the chocolate in a small bowl balanced over a small saucepan of gently simmering water (make sure the base of the bowl does not touch the water). Stir the chocolate until it's melted, then take it off the heat to cool slightly. Add the egg yolk and stir into the melted chocolate, then gently fold in the cream until velvety.

Beat the egg white to soft peaks. Fold one spoonful of fluffy egg white into the mousse with a metal spoon, then gently fold in the remainder — the secret is to use a light, quick touch.

Spoon into a serving glass or bowl. Cover with plastic wrap and refrigerate for 4 hours, or overnight until set. When you're ready to serve, add a curl of whipped cream and a dusting of cocoa powder.

Makes 1

Banana fritters

35 g (1¼ oz/¼ cup) self-raising flour
2 teaspoons caster (superfine) sugar
½ teaspoon ground cinnamon
1 banana
oil, for deep-frying
ice cream, to serve

Sift the flour and a pinch of salt into a small bowl. Make a well in the centre, and gradually add 60 ml (2 fl oz/ ¼ cup) water while gently whisking, drawing flour in from the sides. Whisk until just combined. Don't worry if the batter looks a bit lumpy. Stand for 30 minutes. Combine the sugar and cinnamon in a bowl and set aside.

Cut the banana in half crossways, slightly on the diagonal. Dip into the batter, using tongs. Quickly drain off any excess batter and deep-fry for 2 minutes, or until crisp and golden. Use a slotted spoon to lift the cooked fritters onto paper towels to drain. Sprinkle with the cinnamon sugar and serve with ice cream.

Serves 1

Chocolate croissant pudding

1 croissant, torn into pieces
30 g (1 oz) good-quality dark chocolate, chopped into pieces
1 egg
1½ tablespoons caster (superfine) sugar
60 ml (2 fl oz/¼ cup) milk
60 ml (2 fl oz/¼ cup) cream
1 teaspoon orange liqueur
½ teaspoon grated orange zest
1 tablespoon orange juice
½ tablespoon roughly chopped hazelnuts
cream, to serve

Preheat the oven to 180°C (350°F/Gas 4). Grease base and side of a small heatproof deep-sided ceramic dish (one that will fit into the croissant pieces). Place croissant pieces in the dish, then scatter over about three-quarters of the chocolate pieces.

Beat the egg and sugar together in a small bowl until pale and creamy. Heat milk, cream, liqueur and remaining chocolate in a small saucepan until almost boiling. Stir to melt chocolate, then remove the pan from the heat. Gradually add to the egg mixture, stirring constantly. Next, stir in the orange zest and juice. Slowly pour the mixture over the croissant, allowing the liquid to be fully absorbed before adding more.

Sprinkle hazelnuts over the top and bake for 30 minutes, or until a skewer comes out clean when inserted into the centre. Cool for 10 minutes. Serve warm with a dollop of cream.

Serves 1

Eton mess

1–2 ready-made meringues
4–5 strawberries, hulled
1 teaspoon caster (superfine) sugar
60 ml (2 fl oz/¼ cup) thick (double/ heavy) cream

Break the meringues into pieces. Cut the strawberries into quarters and put them in a bowl with the sugar. Using a potato masher or the back of a spoon, squash them slightly so they start to become juicy. Whip cream in a small bowl with a balloon or electric whisk until it is thick but not solid.

Mix everything together gently and spoon it into a glass.

Serves 1

Lemon pudding with citrus cream

20 g (¾ oz) butter, softened
1½ tablespoons caster (superfine) sugar
½ teaspoon grated lemon zest
1 egg, separated
1 tablespoon self-raising flour
2 tablespoons milk
1 tablespoon lemon juice

Citrus cream
2 tablespoons thick (double/heavy) cream
2 teaspoons icing (confectioners') sugar
¼ teaspoon grated orange zest
¼ teaspoon grated lime zest

Preheat oven to 180°C (350°F/Gas 4). Lightly grease a 250 ml (9 fl oz/1 cup) round ovenproof or soufflé dish. Put the butter, sugar and lemon zest in a small bowl and beat until it is light and well combined.

Add egg yolk and beat well. Add the flour and milk to make a smooth but not runny batter. Stir in lemon juice. The batter may look to have separated at this stage, but this is fine.

In a separate small bowl, whisk the egg white until firm (but not dry) peaks form, then use a metal spoon to gently fold it into the batter. Pour the batter into the ovenproof dish and place into a small roasting tin. Fill the tin with enough boiling water to come one-third of the way up the outside of the dish. Cook for 20–25 minutes, or until risen and firm to the touch. Allow to stand for 10 minutes before serving.

Meanwhile, make the citrus cream. In a small bowl, combine the cream with the sugar and the orange and lime zest. Dust the pudding with icing sugar, if you like, and serve with the citrus cream.

Serves 1

Spiced fruit salad

60 g (2 oz/¼ cup) caster (superfine) sugar
2 slices fresh ginger
small piece bird's eye chilli
juice and zest of 1 lime
fruit, a mixture of watermelon, melon, mango, banana, cherries, lychees, kiwi fruit, or anything else you fancy – enough for 1 portion

Note: Any leftover syrup can be kept covered in the refrigerator for a week.

Put the sugar in a small saucepan with 60 ml (2 fl oz/¼ cup) water and the ginger and chilli. Heat it until the sugar melts, then leave it to cool before adding the lime juice and zest. Take out the ginger and chilli.

Put your selection of fruit into a bowl and pour enough of the syrup over it to coat the fruit. Leave it to marinate in the fridge for 30 minutes. Serve with coconut ice cream or any other kind of ice cream or sorbet.

Serves 1

Crème caramel

2 tablespoons caster (superfine) sugar
250 ml (9 fl oz/1 cup) milk
½ teaspoon natural vanilla extract
2 tablespoons caster (superfine) sugar
1 egg
1 egg yolk

To make the caramel, put the sugar in a small heavy-based saucepan and heat until it dissolves and starts to caramelize — tip the saucepan from side to side as the sugar cooks to keep the colouring even. Remove from the heat and immediately pour into two 200 ml (7 fl oz) ramekins.

Preheat the oven to 180°C (350°F/Gas 4). Put the milk and vanilla extract in a small saucepan and bring just to the boil. Mix together the sugar, egg and egg yolk in a bowl. Pour the boiling milk over the egg mixture and stir well. Ladle into the ramekins and place in a roasting tin. Pour enough hot water into the tin to come halfway up the sides of the ramekins. Cook for 30–35 minutes, or until firm to the touch. Remove from the tin and leave for 15 minutes. For a single serve, unmould one onto a plate and pour on any leftover caramel.

Makes 2

Note: Leave the remaining crème caramel unmoulded in the refrigerator. When required, unmould and serve. It will keep for up to 2 days.

Zuppa inglese

1 thick slice sponge or madeira (pound) cake
2 teaspoons kirsch
a handful of raspberries
a handful of blackberries
2 teaspoons caster (superfine) sugar
80 ml (2½ fl oz/⅓ cup) bought custard
thick cream, to dollop
icing (confectioners') sugar, to dust

Put a piece of sponge cake onto a deep serving plate and either sprinkle or brush with the kirsch. Leave the kirsch to soak in for at least a minute or two.

Put the raspberries and blackberries in a small saucepan with the caster sugar. Gently warm through over a low heat so that the sugar just melts, then leave the fruit to cool.

Spoon the fruit over the sponge, pour the custard on top of the fruit and, finally, dollop the cream on top and dust with icing sugar.

Serves 1

Mango fool

flesh from a large ripe mango
80 ml (2½ fl oz/⅓ cup) Greek-style yoghurt
1 tablespoon thick (double/heavy) cream

Take the flesh off the mango. The easiest way to do this is to slice down either side of the stone so you have 'two cheeks'. Make crisscross cuts through the mango flesh on each cheek, almost through to the skin, then turn each cheek inside out and slice the flesh from the skin into a bowl. Cut any remaining flesh from the mango stone.

Purée flesh by using a food processor or blender, or if you don't have any of these, just mash the flesh thoroughly.

Put a spoonful of mango purée in the bottom of a small glass, bowl or cup, followed by a spoonful of yoghurt on top. Repeat until the mango and the yoghurt are used up. Spoon cream over the top. Swirl the layers together just before you eat them.

Serves 1

Tiramisù

1 egg, separated
1½ tablespoons caster (superfine) sugar
75 g (2½ oz/⅓ cup) mascarpone cheese
60 ml (2 fl oz/¼ cup) cold very strong coffee
1 tablespoon brandy or sweet Marsala
10 small sponge fingers
dark chocolate, finely grated, to dust

In a small bowl beat the egg yolk with the sugar until the sugar has dissolved and the mixture is light and fluffy and leaves a ribbon trail when dropped from the whisk. Add the mascarpone and beat until the mixture is smooth. Whisk the egg white in a clean dry glass bowl until soft peaks form. Fold into the mascarpone mixture.

Pour the coffee into a shallow dish and add the brandy. Dip half of the sponge finger biscuits into the coffee mixture. The biscuits should be fairly well soaked on both sides but not so much so that they break up. Arrange the biscuits in one tightly packed layer over the base of a serving dish that fits the biscuits snugly.

Spread half of the mascarpone mixture over the layer of biscuits. Dip the remaining biscuits in the coffee mixture and add another layer of soaked biscuits and then another layer of mascarpone, smoothing the top layer neatly. Leave to rest in the fridge for at least 2 hours or overnight. Dust with the grated chocolate to serve.

Serves 1

Panna cotta

250 ml (9 fl oz/1 cup) thick (double/heavy) cream
2 tablespoons caster (superfine) sugar
1 tablespoon grappa (grape-based brandy, optional)
natural vanilla extract
1½ leaves or ¾ teaspoon powdered gelatine
fresh berries, to serve

Note: Refrigerate the remaining panna cotta for the next day and unmould when ready to serve.

Put cream and sugar in a saucepan and stir over gentle heat until the sugar has dissolved. Bring to the boil, then simmer for 3 minutes, adding the grappa and a few drops of vanilla extract to taste.

If you are using the gelatine leaves, soak them in cold water until floppy, then squeeze out any excess water. Stir leaves into hot cream until they are completely dissolved. If you are using powdered gelatine, sprinkle it onto hot cream in an even layer and leave it to sponge for a minute, then stir it into the cream until dissolved.

Pour the mixture into two 170 ml (5½ fl oz/⅔ cup) metal or ceramic ramekins, cover each with a piece of plastic wrap and refrigerate until set.

For one serve, unmould one panna cotta by placing the ramekin very briefly in a bowl of hot water and then tipping it gently onto a serving plate. The metal ramekin will take a shorter time than the ceramic to unmould as it heats up more quickly. Serve with the fresh berries.

Makes 2

Chocolate pudding

40 g (1½ oz) dark chocolate, chopped
butter, for greasing
1 tablespoon caster (superfine) sugar
15 g (½ oz) milk chocolate, chopped
1 egg, separated
cream, to serve

Preheat the oven to 200°C (400°F/ Gas 6). Put the dark chocolate in a small glass bowl and set it above a small pan of simmering water. The chocolate will gradually start to soften and look glossy — when it does this, stir it until it is smooth.

Grease the inside of a 200 ml (7 fl oz) ramekin with butter. Add ½ teaspoon of the sugar and shake it around until the inside is coated. Add the chopped milk chocolate to the ramekin.

Beat the rest of the sugar with the egg yolk, using electric beaters or a whisk, for about a minute, or until you have a pale, creamy mass. Clean the beaters or whisk and dry them thoroughly. Whisk the egg white until it is thick enough to stand up in peaks.

Fold the melted chocolate into the yolk mixture and then fold in the beaten egg white. Use a large spoon or rubber spatula to do this and try not to squash out too much air. Spoon mixture into ramekin. Put on a small tray and bake for 15 minutes or until the pudding is puffed and spongelike. Serve immediately with cream.

Serves 1

Sticky black rice pudding with mangoes

100 g (3½ oz/½ cup) black sticky rice
1 piece of fresh pandanus leaf
125 ml (4 fl oz/½ cup) coconut milk
1 tablespoon grated palm sugar
1 teaspoon caster (superfine) sugar
coconut cream, to serve
mango or papaya cubes, to serve

Put the rice in a medium glass or ceramic bowl and cover with water. Leave to soak for at least 8 hours, or overnight. Drain, then put in a small saucepan with 250 ml (9 fl oz/1 cup) of water and slowly bring to the boil. Cook at a slow boil, stirring frequently, for 20 minutes, or until tender. Drain.

Shred the pandanus leaf piece with your fingers, then tie in a knot. Pour coconut milk into a small saucepan and heat until almost boiling. Add the palm sugar, caster sugar and pandanus leaf and stir until the sugar is dissolved.

Add the rice to the pan and cook, stirring, for about 8 minutes without boiling. Remove from the heat, cover and leave for 15 minutes to absorb the flavours. Remove the pandanus leaf.

Serve warm with coconut cream and fresh mango or papaya cubes.

Serves 1

Note: Keep any leftover rice pudding covered in the refrigerator for up to 3 days.

Coffee gelato

5 egg yolks
115 g (3¾ oz/½ cup) caster (superfine) sugar
500 ml (17 fl oz/2 cups) milk
125 ml (4 fl oz/½ cup) freshly made espresso
1 tablespoon Tia Maria or coffee liqueur

Whisk the egg yolks and half the sugar in a bowl until you have a pale and creamy mixture. Pour the milk and coffee into a saucepan, add the remaining sugar and bring to the boil. Add to the egg mixture and whisk together. Pour back into the saucepan and cook over low heat, taking care that the custard doesn't boil. Stir constantly until the mixture is thick enough to coat the back of a wooden spoon. Strain the custard into a bowl and cool over ice before adding the Tia Maria.

To make the gelato by hand, pour the mixture into a freezer-proof container, cover and freeze. Break up the ice crystals every 30 minutes with a fork to ensure a smooth texture. Repeat until it is ready — this may take 4 hours. If using an ice cream machine, follow the manufacturer's instructions.

For a single serve, spoon 1–2 scoops into a serving glass or bowl and freeze the remainder in an airtight container for up to a month.

Makes about 4 cups

Apple crumble

2 apples
1½ tablespoons caster (superfine) sugar
½ teaspoon lemon zest
30 g (1 oz) butter, cubed
35 g (1¼ oz/¼ cup) plain (all-purpose) flour
pinch of ground cinnamon
cream, to serve

Turn oven to 180°C (350°/Gas 4). Peel and core apples, then cut them into chunks. Put apple, lemon zest and half a tablespoon of sugar in a small baking dish and mix together.

In a small bowl, combine the butter and flour and rub them together until you have a texture that resembles coarse breadcrumbs. Stir in the rest of the sugar and the cinnamon. Sprinkle over a teaspoon of water and stir the crumbs together so they form bigger clumps.

Scatter the crumble mixture over the apple and bake the crumble for 45–50 minutes, by which time the top should be browned and the juice bubbling up through the crumble. Serve with cream.

Serves 1

Fruit poached in red wine

1 small pear, peeled, quartered and cored
1 small apple, peeled, quartered and cored
1 tablespoon sugar
¼ vanilla pod, cut in half lengthways
small piece cinnamon stick
125 ml (4 fl oz/½ cup) red wine
60 ml (2 fl oz/¼ cup) dessert wine or port
2 red-skinned plums, halved and stoned
cream or ice cream, to serve

Note: Leftover fruit can be kept covered and refrigerated for up to 3 days.

Put the pear and apple in a medium saucepan. Add the sugar, vanilla pod, cinnamon stick, red wine and dessert wine and bring to the boil. Reduce the heat and gently simmer for about 5–10 minutes, or until just soft.

Add the plums, stirring them through the pears and apples, and bring the liquid back to a simmer. Cook for another 5 minutes, or until the plums are soft.

Remove the saucepan from the heat, cover with a lid and leave the fruit to marinate in the syrup for at least 6 hours. Remove vanilla pod and cinnamon stick. Reheat gently to serve warm or serve at room temperature with cream or ice cream and a biscuit.

Serves 1

Coffee granita

55 g (2 oz/¼ cup) caster (superfine) sugar
310 ml (10¾ fl oz/1¼ cup) very strong espresso coffee
ice cream, to serve

Heat caster sugar with a tablespoon of hot water in a small saucepan until sugar dissolves. Simmer for 3 minutes to make a sugar syrup. Add the coffee and stir well.

Pour into a small plastic or metal freezer box. The mixture should be no deeper than 3 cm (1¼ inches) so that the granita freezes quickly and breaks up easily. Stir every 2 hours with a fork to break up the ice crystals as they form. Repeat this two or three times. The granita is ready when almost set but still grainy. Stir a fork through it just before serving. Spoon into a glass or bowl and serve with ice cream.

Serves 1

Venetian rice pudding

375 ml (13 fl oz/1½ cups) milk
125 ml (4 fl oz/½ cup) thick (double/heavy) cream
½ vanilla pod, split
pinch of ground cinnamon
1 tablespoon caster (superfine) sugar
pinch grated nutmeg
1 teaspoon grated orange zest
40 g (1½ oz/⅓ cup) sultanas (golden raisins)
1 tablespoon brandy or sweet Marsala
55 g (2 oz/¼ cup) risotto or pudding rice

Note: Store any leftover rice pudding covered in the refrigerator for up to 3 days.

Put the milk, thick cream and vanilla pod in a heavy-based saucepan, and bring it just to the boil, then remove from the heat. Add the cinnamon, sugar, nutmeg and orange zest, and set aside.

Put the sultanas and brandy in a small bowl and leave to soak. Add the rice to the infused milk and return to the heat. Bring to a simmer and stir slowly for 30 minutes, or until the rice is creamy. Stir in the sultanas and remove the vanilla pod at the end of cooking. For a single serve, spoon a portion into a serving bowl. Serve warm or cold.

Serves 1

Chocolate affogato

80 g (2¾ oz) dark chocolate
330 ml (11¼ fl oz/1⅓ cups) milk
2 eggs
1½ tablespoons caster (superfine) sugar
125 ml (4 fl oz/½ cup) thick (double/heavy) cream

To serve
1 small cup of espresso or very strong coffee
1 shot Frangelico or any other liqueur that you like

Break the chocolate into individual squares and put it with the milk in a small saucepan. Heat the milk over low heat — you must do this slowly or the chocolate will catch on the bottom. As the milk heats up and the chocolate melts, stir the mixture until you have a smooth liquid. You don't need to boil the milk, as the chocolate will melt at a much lower temperature. Whisk the eggs and sugar together with electric beaters, in a small glass or metal bowl, until the mixture is pale and frothy. Add the milk and chocolate mixture, along with the cream, and mix.

Pour the mixture into a shallow plastic or metal container and put it in the freezer. In order to make a smooth ice cream you will now have to whisk the mixture every hour or so to break up the ice crystals as they form. When the mixture gets very stiff, leave it to set overnight. If using an ice cream machine, follow the manufacturer's instructions. To make a single serve, scoop a ball of the ice cream out of the container and put into a serving cup, then put in the freezer while you make the coffee.

Serve the ice cream with the coffee and Frangelico poured over it.

Makes about 4 cups

Note: The ice cream can be stored in the freezer for up to a month.

Grilled mango cheeks with coconut ice cream

170 ml (5½ fl oz/⅔ cup) vanilla ice cream, softened
1 tablespoon shredded coconut, toasted
2 ripe mango cheeks (from a medium mango)
1 teaspoon soft brown sugar
½ lime

Mix the ice cream and coconut together in a large bowl, stirring only until just combined. Do not allow the ice cream to melt too much or it will become too icy. Return the mixture to a small container and refreeze for an hour until firm.

Preheat a barbecue hotplate, grill plate or chargrill pan to medium. If you prefer to serve mango cheeks without their skin, scoop the cheeks away from the skin using a large spoon, then sprinkle with the sugar. Alternatively, leave the skin on and score flesh in a criss-cross pattern, then sprinkle the flesh with sugar. Put the mango cheeks flesh-side-down on the barbecue and grill for 1–2 minutes, or until the sugar has caramelized. Put the cheeks onto a serving plate and drizzle with a squeeze of lime. Add a scoop or two of the coconut ice cream and serve.

Tip: Coconut ice cream is delicious served with any fruit combination. Try pineapple and bananas for a tropical flavour hit.

Serves 1

Sweet drunken pineapple

¼ large pineapple or ½ small pineapple, quartered
oil, for brushing
1 tablespoon coarsely grated palm sugar or soft brown sugar
1 tablespoon rum
3 teaspoons lime juice
few small mint leaves
thick (double/heavy) cream, to serve

Preheat a barbecue grill plate or chargrill pan (griddle) to medium. Trim the ends from the pineapple quarters and remove the skin. Brush the hot grill plate or chargrill pan with oil, add the pineapple quarters and cook for about 10 minutes, turning to brown the cut sides.

Take the pineapple off the heat and cut into 1.5 cm (½ inch) thick slices. Overlap slices on a small serving plate.

Combine the sugar, rum and lime juice in a small jug, mixing well to dissolve the sugar. Pour the mixture evenly over the warm pineapple slices, then cover with plastic wrap and refrigerate for several hours. Serve at room temperature, sprinkled with the mint leaves and a dollop of cream.

Serves 1

Figs with amaretto mascarpone

Amaretto mascarpone
60 g (2 oz/¼ cup) mascarpone cheese
2 teaspoons icing (confectioners') sugar
2 teaspoons amaretto liqueur or other almond liqueur

1 tablespoon ground almonds
1teaspoon demerara or soft brown sugar
pinch ground cinnamon
2 fresh figs, halved

To make the amaretto mascarpone, put the mascarpone, icing sugar and amaretto in a small bowl and mix together well. Cover and refrigerate for 15 minutes, or until cold.

Heat grill (broiler) to high. In a small bowl, mix together ground almonds, sugar and cinnamon. Sit the fig halves on grill tray and sprinkle with almond mixture. Grill for 3–4 minutes, or until figs are hot, the sugar has melted and tops are lightly browned. Serve hot, dolloped with the chilled mascarpone

Serves 1

Caramelized pears

- 2 ripe corella pears, or other small sweet pears (see Note)
- 1½ tablespoons demerara or soft brown sugar
- 1 tablespoon butter, softened
- 2 teaspoons brandy
- crème fraîche, to serve
- lemon wedge, to serve

Heat the grill (broiler) to high. Peel the pears and halve from top to bottom, keeping stems intact if possible. Core pears using a melon baller or a spoon.

Mix the sugar and butter together in a small bowl, then stir in the brandy. Sit pears, cut-side-down, on the grill tray, and brush the tops with some sugar mixture. Grill for about 5 minutes, or until lightly browned.

Turn pears, brush with a little more sugar mixture, then fill the cavities with remaining mixture. Grill for another 3 minutes, or until sugar is bubbling and brown. Baste again, then grill for a further 3 minutes.

Remove from heat and leave the pears for 5 minutes, then serve with a scoop of crème fraîche, a squeeze of lemon juice and any juices from the grill tray.

Note: If you are unable to obtain small pears, you can use a larger pear and increase the cooking time slightly.

Serves 1

French toast with vanilla yoghurt and fresh mango

1 thick slice two-day old brioche or panettone (see Note)
1 egg
1½ tablespoons milk
1 teaspoon unsalted butter
1 mango cheek, peeled and sliced
good-quality vanilla yoghurt, to serve
¼ teaspoon finely shredded lime zest

Preheat barbecue hotplate or chargrill pan (griddle) to medium. Put the bread in a shallow dish large enough to hold the bread slice. In a small bowl, whisk egg and milk until well combined, then pour mixture over bread and allow to soak for about 3 minutes.

Melt butter on the hotplate or chargrill pan. When hot add the bread slice and fry for 1–2 minutes on each side, or until golden brown. Transfer to a serving plate. Arrange mango slices on top, add a dollop of yoghurt and sprinkle with lime zest and serve.

Note: This is a great way to use up stale or leftover brioche or panettone. Bread should not be soft, otherwise it will become too mushy after grilling.

Serves 1

Basics

Kitchen equipment

Stocking a kitchen is a personal thing based on how much cooking, and what kind of cooking, you like to do. It is not always necessary to buy a whole set of knives — instead, it is better to have a few good ones that will last. Similarly, buy two or three good-quality saucepans and frying pans rather than a whole set of inferior ones. Kitchen equipment can be built up over time.

Basic knives

Kitchen knives Buy the best you can afford. Make sure they are comfortable to hold and that the handle and blade are well balanced. Put them in a block to keep them sharp — if they bash around against things in a drawer they will blunt quickly. You will need one large knife for chopping, one medium all-purpose knife, and one small serrated knife for fruit and tomatoes — if you can, find one with a pointed end that will easily pierce the skins. A serrated bread knife is used for slicing bread. A flat-bladed knife is not a good substitute as it squashes the loaf rather than cuts. Use a steel to keep all your knife edges sharp; ideally, sharpen before every use.

Scissors Kitchen scissors should have tough blades, preferably with a serrated edge. The lower handle should be large enough to grip with three fingers. Poultry shears have a cutting point near the pivot for gripping bones as you cut them.

Specialist knives

Specialist knives These are needed if you plan on being more adventurous with your cooking. A mezzaluna (meaning 'half moon') is a double-handled knife with one or two curved blades. It is rocked from side to side to chop herbs. An oyster knife is essential for opening oysters and other shellfish. Its short, flat blade with two cutting edges slides easily between shells. Basic meat preparation requires a boning knife with a very strong, thin blade. A citrus zester and canelle knife easily peel off zest using a row of small holes or a deeper, V-shaped cutting edge.

Saucepans and frying pans

Saucepans These should be good quality and the most expensive ones that you can afford. There is a huge range on the market but stainless steel with a sandwich base (stainless steel sandwiching a metal such as copper that conducts heat well) are a good bet for even heat distribution. Stainless steel is also non-reactive (that is, it is not affected by the use of an acid such as lemon juice, which can cause a chemical reaction and taint the food). Choose pans with comfortable handles (check they do not heat up) and lids that have a tight seal. You will need one large pan and a couple of smaller ones. A pasta boiler with a fitted drainer is useful for cooking pasta.

Frying pans Like saucepans, these should be good quality. Cast-iron ones are heavy but last a very long time. Non-stick ones have to be used with wooden or plastic implements. An ovenproof handle is useful for making anything that needs to be finished in the oven or under a grill (broiler).

Ovenware

Ovenware These should be good quality and be able to be used on the stovetop and in the oven. Casseroles need to be heavy enough to absorb and retain heat and also need tight-fitting lids so as not to let any moisture escape. Cast-iron or enamelled ones (with cast-iron or steel underneath) are generally the best as they conduct heat well. You will need several sizes as it is important that the recipe fits the casserole. Baking and gratin dishes should be fully ovenproof and able to withstand high heat. Enamel, cast-iron and stoneware are good options.

Roasting tins These should be made from stainless steel or anodized aluminium so the tins can be used over a heat source without buckling. Ones that have a rack are particularly useful, as meat and poultry can be roasted and the fat and juices collected underneath.

General equipment

Chopping board An essential, whether wooden or polyethylene. Your board should be kept spotlessly clean. It's a good idea to have one for meat, poultry and fish and another for all other items.

Graters These vary in shape, but the important part is the cutting edge; it should be very sharp. A box grater is good for large quantities and doesn't slip easily.

Potato masher Potato mashers work on all cooked vegetables. Old-style mashers with a cut grid are very good.

Tin opener It is worth buying a good-quality one that grips properly.

Juice squeezer Available in glass, ceramic, plastic and wood. Those with a container underneath for collecting the juice are the most useful.

Sieves These come in a range of sizes. Larger colanders are best for draining. Round-bottomed stainless steel sieves have a mesh suitable for sifting and puréeing and nylon mesh sieves are for fine sifting and puréeing.

Kitchen utensils

Spoons Useful for stirring, mixing and beating. Wooden spoons are good because they do not conduct heat, do not scratch and are non-reactive. Metal spoons are used for folding ingredients. A perforated spoon is useful for draining. Ladles are made for serving liquids.

Pastry brush Made with either nylon or natural bristles and can be flat or round.

Peeler A good peeler shaves only a thin skin off vegetables.

Rubber spatula This can scrape a bowl completely clean.

Fish slice This needs enough flexibility to be able to slide under things.

Asian equipment

Wok Buy a carbon steel or pressed steel wok from your local Chinatown as they conduct heat better. Season by rubbing it with salt and hot oil, then wipe it out after each use rather than washing it — this will build up a non-stick surface over time. Use with a wok charn for stir-frying. This is a shovel-like spatula ideal for tossing food around the curved side of the wok.

Chopper/cleaver Used for chopping through bones. Buy a heavy one for chopping and a lighter one for slicing.

Metal or bamboo tongs These are very useful for turning things over, or lifting things out of boiling liquids.

Clay pot Glazed on the inside, a clay pot is used for slow cooking as it heats up evenly all over.

Steamers Bamboo stackable steamers are simple to use and inexpensive.

Specialist equipment

Mortar and pestle This comprises a bowl (mortar) with a slightly rough surface and a crushing 'stick' (pestle) that fits the curvature of the bowl and provides the second grinding surface. Purchase a large, heavy one for multiple ingredients. They are good for crushing seeds, spices and cloves of garlic.

Salt and pepper mills (grinders) A steel grinding mechanism is efficient.

Scales, measuring cups and thermometers

Scales You only need one good-quality set of scales with highly visible measurement indicators. Choose one with both metric and imperial weights.

Measuring jugs Plastic and glass jugs are best as you can read them easily. Choose one with very clear calibrations.

Measuring cups Often used instead of scales for dry and liquid measures. Available in fractions and multiples of cup measures.

Measuring spoons These are available in sets ranging from ¼ teaspoon to 1 tablespoon. For accuracy, dry measurements should be levelled off with a knife.

Thermometers Buy one type to measure oil temperatures accurately, and an oven thermometer to ensure that the thermostat is registering correctly. This is particularly important when baking cakes and cookies.

Grocery shopping

Like equipment, ingredients should always be the best you can afford. There is no point in paying less and having an inferior product. For fresh goods, buy little and often. While a bulk purchase may seem economical, it can cost you in the long run if you don't use it all while it is still in premium condition and you have to discard some. Frequent your local farmers' market for fresh fruit and vegetables and always buy in season. The quality will be better and the price more reasonable.

Storage

Storing groceries properly will keep them in better condition for longer. You'll find more information on this topic in a chart opposite. Delicate herbs and young salad leaves can be stored for a few days in the refrigerator wrapped in damp paper towels. Use them as quickly as possible. Root vegetables are best kept in the crisper drawer of the fridge. Keep tomatoes in a basket or bowl near a natural light source. Apples and citrus fruits should be kept separate from other fruits as they speed up their ripening process.

If you loosely cover meat or fish with plastic wrap and place it on a plate, it will keep for 1-2 days in the fridge. Never place meat, poultry or fish where the juices can drip onto other ingredients and contaminate them.

Freezing

Ingredients that you don't immediately need for cooking can be placed in the freezer. Freezing is also a great way to store leftovers for later consumption.
A thermometer inside the freezer should allow you to monitor the ideal constant temperature of –18 °C. To ensure all the food freezes evenly, don't fill the freezer beyond 75 per cent capacity. Always put the food you are freezing into freezer bags or it will dry out. Label the bags clearly with the date and its contents.

Never re-freeze food that has been defrosted. Frozen food should be thawed in the refrigerator or somewhere cool. Never thaw in proximity to a heat source. Milk and cream are not suitable for freezing as the whey will split upon thawing. Never freeze meals that contain mayonnaise or raw eggs.

FOOD	REFRIGERATOR	FREEZER (3-star-section)
dairy & eggs		
butter	2 weeks	6 months
buttermilk	1 week	
eggs	3 weeks	
cream cheese	1 week	
cheese	10 days	3–6 months
yoghurt	2 weeks	
milk	1 week	
cream	2 weeks	
sour cream	2 weeks	
vegetables, fruits & herbs		
eggplant (aubergines)	5–7 days	-
berries	2–3 days	-
cauliflower	1 week	-
broccoli	5 days	-
cucumber	1 week	-
herbs	3–4 days	-
pumpkin (squash)	1–2 weeks	-
carrots	1–2 weeks	-
capsicum (bell peppers)	1 week	-
mushrooms	2–3 days	-
salad	2–3 days	-
zucchini (courgettes)	5–7 days	-
fish & meat		
fish, raw	1–2 days	3 months
poultry, meat, raw	2–3 days	3–6 months
mince (ground meat), raw	1–2 days	3 months
salami	1 week	3 months
ham	1 week	3 months
sausages	5 days	3 months
cooked food		
poultry, pieces, cooked	1–2 days	1 month (3 to 6, in sauce)
pasta	2–3 days	
potatoes	2–3 days	
rice	1–2 days	
soups and stews	2–3 days	1–3 months
casseroles	2–3 days	1 month

Cookery Terms

al dente Italian phrase meaning 'to the tooth'. Refers to pasta and sometimes vegetables. Means slightly underdone, so still with some 'bite'.

bain-marie Also called a 'water bath'. Usually a baking dish half-filled with water so delicate food is protected from direct heat. Often used for custards.

bake blind To bake an empty pastry case before the filling is added. Ensures the pastry is cooked through and not soggy. The case is usually lined with baking paper and with baking beads, rice or beans, so it keeps its shape.

baste To spoon or brush cooking juices over food during cooking.

boil To cook liquid, or food in liquid, at 100°C (212°F). Large bubbles will break on the surface.

bouquet garni A small bunch of herbs used to flavour stocks, soups and stews. Removed before serving.

brown To fry food (usually meat) fast so the outside is cooked and has changed colour, usually to a golden brown.

cream To beat butter or butter and sugar together until light and creamy.

cube To chop food into even cubes so that it cooks evenly.

dice To chop food into very small even cubes.

drain To remove liquid from food, (usually with a colander or sieve). Individual recipes will state whether the liquid needs to be kept for another stage of the preparation.

en croute Cooked entirely encased in pastry. Usually refers to meat.

escalope Very thin slice of meat, such as veal or chicken.

fillet To cut meat/fish from the bones.

flambé To pour liqueur over food (usually in the pan, over heat) and set it alight to burn off the alcohol and caramelise the sugar content.

fold To mix one ingredient into another very gently (usually flour or egg whites) with a metal spoon or plastic spatula. The idea is to combine the mixture without losing the air. To fold properly, cut through the centre of the mixture, then run the edge of the spoon or spatula around the outer edge of the bowl, turning the bowl as you go.

glaze A substance (often warmed jam or beaten egg) brushed over food to give it shine and colour.

grease To lightly coat a tin or dish with oil or melted butter to prevent food sticking.

infuse To flavour a liquid by heating it with aromatic ingredients (often spices) and leaving it to let the flavour develop.

julienne To cut into uniform thin matchsticks for quick cooking. Often used for stir-fries or in French cuisine.

knead To stretch and fold dough to make it firm and smooth. This stretches the gluten in the flour and gives the dough elasticity. Used for bread making but not for pastry making; overhandling pastry makes it tough.

marinate To tenderize and flavour food, most often meat, fish or poultry, by leaving it in an acidulated, seasoned liquid (a marinade) for minutes or hours.

parboil To cook partially in boiling water before some other form of cooking. Most commonly used for roast potatoes which can be parboiled before being added to the roasting meat.

pinch A small amount of something—as much as can be held between your thumb and forefinger.

poach To cook food immersed in a gently simmering liquid.

punch down the dough A term used in bread making. A yeast dough which is left to rise is then punched with one firm blow of the fist, to remove the air from it.

purée Food blended or processed to a pulp.

reduce To boil or simmer liquid in an uncovered pan so that the liquid evaporates and the mixture becomes thicker and more concentrated in flavour. Most soups and stews are reduced—this should usually be done at a simmer so the flavour of the dish is not impaired by long, hard boiling.

roux The basic mixture of many sauces—fat (usually melted butter) and flour. Used to thicken. Liquid is added to make a sauce.

score To ensure even cooking. Make incisions with a knife that do not cut all the way through.

sift To shake dry ingredients (such as flour or cocoa powder) through a sieve to aerate and remove lumps.

simmer To cook liquid, or food in liquid, over low heat, below boiling point. The surface of the liquid will be moving with a few small bubbles.

skim To remove fat or scum that comes to the surface of a liquid.

soft peaks A term used when egg whites are whipped. The peak will fold over on itself when the beater is lifted.

stiff peaks A term used when egg whites are whipped. The peak will hold its shape when the beater is lifted.

stir-fry To quickly fry (usually in a wok) over high heat while stirring.

strain To remove any solids from a liquid by pouring it through a sieve. The solids are discarded, unless specified.

whisk To beat rapidly with a wire or electric whisk, to incorporate air and add volume.

zest The coloured outer skin of citrus fruits. Avoid the bitter white pith below.

Pasta Basics

There are good reasons why pasta is such a popular food: it's cheap, it's quick and easy to prepare, it's delicious, it's nutritious and it's amazingly versatile. And, it's an excellent ingredient for those cooking for one. You can dress up pasta for a dinner party, or serve it simply, with parmesan. You can eat pasta every day of the week and never tire of it. Pasta goes well with anything, including bread, vegetables and salads.

Cooking tips

Pasta should be cooked in a large, deep saucepan of boiling water to allow room for expansion and to prevent it sticking together. Allow about 6 litres (24 cups) of water for every 500 g (1 lb 2 oz) pasta, but generally, don't use less than 4 litres (16 cups). Filled pasta and large pasta, such as lasagne, will need more water (9–12 litres/36–48 cups), as they are more likely to stick. If you need to cook large amounts of pasta, cook up to 1 kg (2 lb 4 oz) of pasta per saucepan.

Always bring the water to the boil before stirring in the pasta. When the water comes back to the boil, begin timing, stirring often once the pasta softens a little. Test the pasta just prior to the final cooking time.

Cooking time

Cooking times for pasta vary depending on its size and shape and whether it is fresh or dried. Generally, the fresher the pasta, the shorter the cooking time. Fresh pasta only needs 1–2 minutes. Vacuum-packed fresh pasta from the supermarket requires a little longer — about 6 minutes. Dried pasta varies depending on the size and shape but because it needs rehydrating as well as cooking, it usually takes longer than fresh pasta.

For the most accurate times for all pasta, follow the packet instructions. The best way to ensure pasta is cooked is to taste it. The pasta should be just tender and slightly resistant to the bite (al dente), not at all raw or soft and gluggy.

Perfect pasta

Once you have established that the pasta is al dente (tender but still firm 'to the tooth'), it is important to drain it and then turn it immediately into a heated dish, into the pan with the sauce, or back into its cooking pan. It should never be overdrained, as it needs to be slippery for the sauce to coat it well. Never leave it sitting in the colander or it will quickly become a sticky mass.

Never rinse the pasta unless stated in the recipe (it is usually only rinsed if used in a baked meal or served cold in a salad) because the starches released in cooking pasta help it meld beautifully with the sauce. A little oil or butter tossed through drained pasta will stop pasta sticking together. Alternatively, lightly spray pasta with some boiling water and toss it gently (it is a good idea to reserve a little cooking water for this, in case you overdrain the pasta).

Pasta that is to be used in cold pasta salads should be rinsed under cold water, then tossed with a small amount of oil. Cover and refrigerate until using.

Timing can make all the difference between a good pasta meal and a great one. Always read the recipe through first and then coordinate your cooking times. Try to have the sauce ready to dress the pasta as soon as it is cooked, especially if pasta is fresh (it will continue to cook if it is left to sit around).

Index

Published in 2011 by Murdoch Books Pty Limited

Murdoch Books Australia
Pier 8/9, 23 Hickson Road
Millers Point NSW 2000
Phone: +61 (0)2 8220 2000
Fax: +61 (0)2 8220 2558
www.murdochbooks.com.au

Murdoch Books UK Limited
Erico House, 6th Floor
93–99 Upper Richmond Road
Putney, London SW15 2TG
Phone: +44 (0)20 8785 5995
Fax: +44 (0)20 8785 5985
www.murdochbooks.co.uk

Chief Executive: Juliet Rogers
Publishing Director: Chris Rennie

Publisher: Lynn Lewis
Senior Designer: Heather Menzies
Photography (cover): Stuart Scott
Stylist (cover): Louise Bickle
Editorial Coordinator: Liz Malcolm
Production: Joan Beal

National Library of Australia Cataloguing-in-Publication entry
Title: Cooking for one. ISBN: 978-1-74196-953-5 (pbk.)
Series: Chunky series. Notes: Includes bibliographical references.
Subjects: Cookery for one. Dewey Number: 641.5611

Printed in China by 1010 Printing International.
Reprinted in 2012.

Cover credits: Lime green dish, Mud Australia. Multi stripe fabric, No Chintz.
Wine glass and orange and mustard stripe fabric, ici et la. White flower side plate, White Home.